FRESH
VEGGIE
KITCHEN

FRESH VEGGIE KITCHEN

NATURAL, NUTRITIOUS AND DELICIOUS WHOLEFOOD RECIPES
TO NOURISH BODY AND SOUL

DAVID & CHARLOTTE BAILEY

PAVILION

CONTENTS

INTRODUCTION

We're so excited to share with you our second book and we hope that it gives you lots of new ideas for vegetarian wholefood meals to be enjoyed time and time again. Eating well is such a vital part of living well and our aim with this book has been to create food that makes you feel happy and feel good, which is what we would wish for you all.

We started our business, Wholefood Heaven, in 2010 – yes, because we fell in love with a Citroën H van and bought it before we'd really thought it through properly, but also because we wanted to show that you can eat vegetarian wholefood and not only thoroughly enjoy the taste, but also feel nourished and good in yourself as a result. The street food scene, which was beginning to hot up then, seemed the perfect way to go. We've been thrilled by how, year on year, more and more people at festivals, events and markets around the country have been so receptive to what we offer. The lovely feedback we get touches our hearts and we're so happy to live in a time where ever greater numbers of people are opening up to the ideas of vegetarianism and to eating foods in their most natural, unprocessed states. It's not just good for you but it's also for the greater good and, from a foodie point of view, you'll discover an incredible array of sustaining and delicious ingredients.

Perhaps we should take a moment to explain what we mean by wholefoods. We interpret them as foods that are as close to their natural form as possible: vegetables, fruits, nuts, seeds, legumes and whole grains, especially those ancient grains that have remained unchanged for thousands of years. And why are they so good? Well, many health experts now agree that eating more wholefoods is one of the best ways forward for living a healthy life and preventing disease. These wholefoods not only retain all their fibre, but they are also packed with vitamins and minerals and valuable phytochemicals that are often removed in processed foods. What's more, they don't subject your system to the countless preservatives and chemicals and excess amounts of refined sugar, salt, and trans fats (look out for products that list partially hydrogenated oils on the label) that are commonly associated with processed

and manufactured foods. That being said, we do allow for the use of some ingredients that have technically been 'processed': after all, even just turning an apple into a juice is a form of processing. To our minds, minimal processing isn't a problem, we just don't want food that's been heavily manipulated or refined or that's full of added salt, sugar, oil, chemicals or preservatives. Get used to reading the ingredients labels and you'll soon get a feel for what's real food and what's been messed around with.

Another focus in this book has been to further explore the concept of bowl food. When we first started Wholefood Heaven, we never would have thought we'd just have one signature dish, but we do, our beloved Buddha bowls, and it works really well. We first heard the term 'Buddha bowl' from an American chef friend of ours and we thought it was a catchy term and a great concept: a bowl filled with your favourite, good-for-you things, put together with love. Some of our favourite things at the time were (and still are, though we've been eating at least two Buddha bowls a week for six years) Massaman curry, short-grain brown rice, carrot and kimchi pickle, flash-steamed curly kale and omega seed sprinkle, so we put them all together and our Buddha bowl was born. We've sold thousands and thousands of them over the years and many people go out of their way to tell us how much they've enjoyed them. They've won awards, been on the television and been featured in countless newspapers and magazines across the world and we think a big part of their popularity is that they're packed full of different flavours and textures but are also nutritionally balanced – just what you need after a few days of swamp living at Glastonbury! We've enjoyed expanding this winning approach and the mains section of this book contains lots of other meals that work around the same concept of getting all your nutrition and an explosive flavour combination in one bowl.

As caterers most often to be found working in a field – and as (in the case of David anyway) slightly frustrated outdoorsmen (this is a man, who, living in the centre of London, asked for a Gränsfors Bruk axe for Christmas) – we have developed a number of recipes that are just begging to be made outdoors over an open flame or a barbecue. It all goes back to living well: for us, time spent together in nature, eating natural food, are our best of times. For these kinds of recipes, we often use our cast-iron skillet and Dutch oven, ideal for

one-pot cooking and the pieces of equipment we usually turn to first. If you don't have these items, all our recipes can be made using a frying pan or a large pot or casserole dish, but they're great things to invest in and even if you don't get to cook outdoors as often as you might like, they're very handy for use in a home kitchen.

We've absolutely loved writing this book, experimenting with new dishes and sharing them with our friends and family and now, best of all, with you.

RECIPE KEY

V = VEGAN
VO = VEGAN OPTION
WF = WHEAT-FREE
GF = GLUTEN-FREE

WHOLEFOOD STORE CUPBOARD

In this book we've tried to go with an everyday eating vibe and to keep the recipes, for the most part, pretty straightforward. While we're always inspired by our travels (the number one perk of running a flexible street food business is being able to plan trips for the quieter times of year) and have certainly drawn on that inspiration, we've also tried, in the main, to keep to ingredients that shouldn't be too difficult to track down. We're so pleased at how larger supermarkets these days stock a huge variety of wholefoods; if you can't find what you want at the supermarket, head to a health food shop and stock up with some of the staples we've listed below. With these in your cupboard, along with lots of fresh fruits and vegetables, you'll be set for wholefood eating for a long time.

WHOLE GRAINS

BARLEY

Barley is the highest in fibre of all the whole grains and is great for cardiovascular health; we often add it to soups, stews or salads. Wholegrain barley is commonly known as hulled barley; pearl, or pearled, barley is more widely available and is quicker to prepare but it is more processed, meaning that a lot of the nutritional elements have been removed. We use barley flakes to make our lemon barley water (page 151) and they're also good for making a quick barley porridge – but try to ensure the flakes are made from hulled (rather than pearled) barley to maximize the benefits.

BUCKWHEAT (KASHA)

Buckwheat (also commonly known as kasha) is a fantastic ingredient, rich in protein. Harvested from the seeds of a flowering plant, it is from a completely different botanical family to regular wheat and so is a great option for those looking for wheat-free and gluten-free choices. It has a very earthy taste and is brilliant in soups, stews and also as a porridge. Popular in Eastern Europe, this was our staple food when we travelled across Russia.

BULGUR

Bulgur is a wholewheat grain that has been cracked and partially pre-cooked, so is quick and easy to prepare. It can be used just like rice or couscous and goes especially well with Middle Eastern flavours.

COUSCOUS

Quick and easy to cook, filling and delicious, this North African staple is used all the time in our house. Our favourite is kamut couscous, which can be found in health food stores (we use the Lima brand). Kamut is a particularly high-protein ancient grain and is otherwise known as Khorasan wheat, referring to the area in modern-day Iran where it was originally cultivated. It's often better tolerated than common wheat and is considered more energizing, but if you can't find it, use wholewheat couscous.

FREEKEH

Freekeh is a brilliant addition to the cupboard: it can be served as a side like rice or quinoa, it can be added to soups, salads or pilafs, and it also makes a mean risotto. It's a hard wheat, usually durum, that is harvested when the plant is still young and green and is then roasted and rubbed, a process that gives it a unique smoky flavour.

MILLET

A health food cliché, millet is perhaps best known as bird seed, but it's a wonderful ingredient to become familiar with. It's such a nutritious grain, packed with vitamins and minerals including magnesium, copper, manganese and phosphorous. You can boil it up to make a fluffy side dish to serve as an alternative to rice or potatoes, and it also makes terrific porridge. We generally toast our millet before we boil it as we find that gives it a better taste, although it's not essential. You can also buy flaked millet, which is a bit quicker to prepare.

OATS

Oats are always good to have at hand for baking or for a quick breakfast. They really do keep you full for a long time and so are a brilliant way to start the day. They are also known to help lower blood pressure and cholesterol. While oats are rarely classified as gluten free as a result of cross contamination with wheat, they are still sometimes better tolerated by those sensitive to gluten and you can find guaranteed gluten-free brands in some shops these days.

QUINOA

A source of complete protein (great for veggies) with a fantastic nutritional profile, and gluten free, quinoa is very often found on our table as a side or in salads. It's actually a pseudo-cereal as it belongs to the same family as chard and spinach, but it's generally consumed in the same way as other grains.

RICE

Short-grain brown rice (our most-used ingredient: so nutty, so chewy), long-grain brown rice (also jolly nice), black rice (looks and tastes amazing), red rice (same), wild rice (actually a grass); all of these are well worth getting to know and love. Loaded with B vitamins and a host of minerals and a great source of fibre and protein, wholegrain rice is also the most easily digested of all the grains.

RYE

Rye has a distinctive malty flavour that we adore, and the type of fibre found in rye makes it especially good for helping you feel full. It's widely used in Nordic countries and Russia because it's able to grow in areas too cold and wet for other grains, but we're very glad word has spread. The grains need to be soaked overnight, so you'll need to plan ahead.

SPELT

Higher in protein than common wheat and anecdotally recognized as often being better tolerated by people with wheat sensitivities, spelt is a grain we use all the time, adding it to soups, stews and salads. Whole spelt grains do take the best part of an hour to cook but they're packed with far more nutrients than the pearled type.

FLOURS

We're never without coconut flour, spelt flour and wholemeal (wholewheat) flour. We also use teff flour to make *injera* (Ethiopian flatbreads – see page 72), and masa harina flour for Mexican cooking.

PULSES/LEGUMES

We always make sure to have lots of pulses and beans in our store cupboard so we can quickly rustle up a healthy meal at any time. We use both dried and canned (our usual preference, as we are a bit lazy), particularly the following: black beans; cannellini beans; chickpeas; red, green and Puy lentils; pinto beans; red kidney beans; yellow split peas – but there are many more to experiment with.

Mixed sprouts are another ingredient we love to have in the fridge to use as a sprinkle. Mung beans, chickpeas, lentils and alfalfa, or a mix of all of them, are the ones we tend to go to first and they're a great way to add protein and a healthy dose of enzymes to meals such as salads, soups and stir-fries. You'll find them ready to use in health food shops and many supermarkets, or you can buy the seeds dry and sprout them yourself at home.

Edamame beans in their pods are a handy snack to keep in the freezer; they're also a super protein boost to add to vegan meals.

NUTS AND SEEDS

We use these all the time; even when the recipe doesn't call for it, we often sprinkle some crushed nuts or seeds over our food. It's an easy way to boost intake of essential fatty acids and get some plant protein.

Almonds, hazelnuts, pecans, cashews and walnuts are the nuts we use most.

We also love making a mixture of omega-3-rich seeds to sprinkle over breakfast cereals, soups, salads and main courses: the mix usually includes golden and brown flaxseeds (also known as linseeds), sesame seeds, sunflower seeds and poppy seeds. Hemp seeds are also great, black sesame seeds look sexy and we don't know how we ever lived without chia seeds (although they need to be soaked or crushed, not just sprinkled).

HERBS AND SPICES

With a few herbs and spices, you can transform a simple can of beans into something special.

Among our favourite herbs are basil, coriander (cilantro), mint, oregano, parsley, rosemary, tarragon and thyme.

The spices we use most often are: cardamom (we tend to use the seeds from whole green cardamom pods: split them open just before you want to use them, scrape out the seeds and discard the pods), cayenne, chilli flakes and whole dried chillies such as chipotle, cinnamon (sticks and ground), cloves, coriander seeds, cumin (seeds and ground), curry leaves, curry powder, kaffir lime leaves, nutmeg, paprika (smoked and sweet), pepper (white and black), saffron, and turmeric.

TOFU AND SOYA CHUNKS

It's easy to get confused by tofu. Fresh, firm, silken, soft, smoked, it certainly comes in many different forms. But if we mention tofu, we usually mean the fresh, firm tofu sold as blocks in water, which you'll find in the chiller cabinets in shops. We love the Clean Bean brand, which is sold in and around London: it's a handmade artisanal product and we like to buy locally made tofu as it's especially fresh. Cauldron and other brands are also good and are widely available.

The other type of tofu we often use is smoked tofu (we love the Taifun brand), which is also found in the chilled section in shops. It's brilliant in stir-fries, stews, sandwiches and salads.

We also use soya chunks all the time; we even put them in our Buddha bowl curry. Yes, they look a bit like dried dog food and probably taste similar if you don't know what you're doing with them, but these are one of our all-time favourite ingredients. You have to soak them in freshly boiled water until they're soft (about 15 minutes), then you simply strain them and they're ready to be added to all kinds of stews and curries to add protein and substance. They take on the flavour of whatever you cook them in and that's what makes them yummy. You'll find them in the dry goods section of any health food shop.

OTHER THINGS

MIRIN

We use this Japanese rice-based cooking wine in sauces, dressings and marinades.

MISO PASTE

We always have a jar of Clearspring's brown rice miso paste in our fridge, which we use for soups, stews, marinades, dressings or as a seasoning. Miso Tasty is another great brand we love to use.

OILS

Coconut oil is a delicious and healthy choice to cook and bake with, especially when making Southeast Asian-inspired meals.

We also use a lot of olive oil and always go for an unfiltered extra virgin oil if possible.

High-quality butter is also something we like to have to hand, as is ghee. Ghee is a delicious Ayurvedic staple and, as the milk proteins are removed, is an ingredient that is sometimes better tolerated by those who struggle with dairy.

We don't cook with toasted sesame oil, but it adds a lovely nutty finish to stir-fries and other dishes and is also great in dressings and dipping sauces.

SEAWEED

Great for your health (being one of the rare vegetarian sources of iodine as well as countless other minerals and vitamins) and great for adding depth to your dishes; we always have some dried seaweeds in our cupboard. Kombu, nori, dulse, wakame and sea vegetable salad are our most used seaweeds.

SWEET STUFF

Rapadura sugar is one of our favourite ways to add a little sweetness. It's an unrefined sugar with a delicious caramel flavour and it can be used in baking and so on in just the same way as regular granulated sugar. Of course it's still sugar and should be enjoyed in moderation, but being unrefined it's a great source of vitamins and minerals. If rapadura is unavailable we often turn to muscovado or other unrefined brown sugars. They also retain far more of their nutrients, as well as a wonderful depth of flavour. Billington's has a great range, available in most supermarkets.

We also use agave, dates (especially medjool), honey, maple syrup, and palm sugar.

TAMARI

We always use this in place of soy sauce. It has a deep flavour and is wheat-free and gluten-free.

VEGETABLE BOUILLON POWDER

Always good to have some of this around if you don't have time to make your own stock.

VINEGARS

Apple cider vinegar is great in dressings and marinades and so good for you, too. Buy an organic unfiltered apple cider vinegar and it will still have traces of the 'mother', a slightly creepy cobwebby thing that contains enzymes and good bacteria, which help to maintain a healthy gut.

Brown rice vinegar has a lovely light flavour that's fab in Asian dishes and salad dressings.

CHAPTER 1
BREAKFASTS
AND BRUNCH

CHIA SEED BIRCHER BOWL

Bircher muesli was first developed in the early 1900s by the Swiss doctor Maximilian Bircher-Benner, a man regarded by many as the father of the raw food movement and certainly one of the first people in Europe to pioneer the inclusion of a high proportion of uncooked food into one's diet. This muesli is a popular breakfast in Switzerland and Germany and it's one of our favourites, too. The chia seeds add an extra boost of protein, fibre and omega 3, among many other nutritional benefits.

It's best if you can soak the oats overnight, and it's an easy thing to knock up before you go to bed, but it's no disaster if you don't – the muesli will still taste good even if you only manage to soak it for 15 minutes or so. And you can really experiment with this breakfast: try soaking the oats in water, milk or apple juice in place of the orange juice, using different dried fruits, stirring in milk or cream instead of yogurt, and topping it with your choice of nuts. It's very hard to make it not taste fabulous and it's a great start to the day!

75g/2½oz/scant 1 cup porridge (rolled) oats

2 tbsp chia seeds

200ml/7fl oz/¾ cup orange juice

30g/1oz/3 tbsp raisins

1 apple, grated

150g/5½oz/⅔ cup natural yogurt

3 strawberries, sliced

15g/½oz/3 tbsp flaked (sliced) almonds

honey, to drizzle

1. Put the oats, chia seeds, orange juice and raisins in a mixing bowl. Cover and place in the fridge to soak, ideally overnight.

2. Stir in the grated apple and then the yogurt. Spoon into bowls. Top with strawberries, flaked almonds and a drizzle of honey.

Vegan option Delicious with plant-based milk or yogurt, and agave or maple syrup in place of honey.

KEDGEREE

SERVES 4
WF / GF

Kedgeree is a great example of an Anglo–Indian dish and it makes a brilliant one-pan breakfast. It originated from the traditional Indian *khichdi*, a dish of split peas and rice that we've included in our soups and stews section (page 56), but the addition of eggs and herbs such as tarragon and parsley (and flaked fish too, of course, in the more traditional version) makes clear the British influence. We love to pimp it up with some grilled halloumi, making it Anglo–Indian–Cypriot!

2 tbsp olive oil

1 onion, chopped

3 garlic cloves, crushed

salt and black pepper

¼ tsp turmeric

½ tsp mild curry powder

300g/10½oz/1½ cups short-grain brown rice

150g/5½oz/¾ cup red lentils

500ml/18fl oz/2 cups vegetable stock

750ml/1¼ pints/3 cups water

2 stems kale, roughly shredded

1 sprig tarragon, leaves plucked and roughly chopped

250g/9oz halloumi, cut into 8 slices (optional)

4 eggs, boiled and cut into quarters

3 sprigs parsley, chopped

1 lemon, cut into 4 wedges

1. Heat the olive oil in a large casserole dish or Dutch oven, add the onion and sauté for a couple of minutes, stirring occasionally. Add the garlic and a pinch of salt and cook for a further couple of minutes. Then stir in the turmeric and curry powder and cook for another minute or so.

2. Add the rice and lentils and pour in the vegetable stock and water, cover and cook over a medium heat for about 30 minutes, stirring occasionally. Turn the heat down if you find it's starting to catch.

3. Remove the lid and cook over a low heat for 5–10 minutes, stirring occasionally, until the rice and lentils are fully cooked and the mixture has dried out a bit. Add the kale and tarragon and continue cooking for a couple of minutes. Season to taste with salt and pepper.

4. If using, place the halloumi slices in a hot pan or skillet and cook until golden on both sides. Remove from the pan, cut into cubes and stir them through the kedgeree.

5. Transfer to serving plates and add one egg to each portion along with some parsley and a wedge of lemon to garnish.

SHAKSHUKA

SERVES 2
WF / GF

We see shakshuka on brunch menus everywhere these days and we're so pleased about that as it's become a favourite; we're even keen to arrange a pilgrimage to Dr Shakshuka, a restaurant down a tiny alley in Jaffa where the speciality is..., you guessed it! A North African dish, shakshuka has many possible variations: try using different herbs and spices or different coloured peppers (or substitute aubergine); leaving out the preserved lemon or garlic (we use both at every opportunity, but it's also good without); adding feta or other cheeses, or even some beans. However you roll, be sure to serve with lots of your favourite bread.

½ tsp cumin seeds
2 tbsp olive oil
1 onion, sliced
2 garlic cloves, crushed
1 red pepper, cut into thick slices
1 green pepper, cut into thick slices
400g (1 can) chopped tomatoes
1 bay leaf
¼ preserved lemon, pulp removed and discarded, skin thinly sliced
handful parsley, chopped
2 tsp unrefined brown sugar
¼ tsp cayenne
pinch of saffron
½ tsp sweet paprika
salt and black pepper
200ml/7fl oz/¾ cup water
4 eggs
handful coriander (cilantro), chopped

1. Heat a skillet or frying pan over a medium heat, add the cumin seeds and dry-roast for 1–2 minutes, shaking the pan occasionally, until they start to release their aroma.

2. Add the olive oil and the onion and sauté over a high heat for 3–5 minutes. Add the garlic and the peppers and cook for a few more minutes, stirring continuously, until the peppers have started to take on a bit of colour.

3. Add the tomatoes, bay leaf, preserved lemon, parsley, sugar, cayenne, saffron, paprika, a pinch of salt and the water. Turn the heat down to medium, cover the skillet with a lid and cook for 12–15 minutes or until the peppers are completely cooked, stirring occasionally and adding a little more water if the mixture seems to be drying out too much. At this stage you want it to be quite saucy.

4. Remove the lid to allow the mixture to thicken slightly, stirring regularly.

5. Turn the heat down as low as possible, make four hollows in the mixture and crack an egg into each hollow. Cover with a lid and cook over a low heat for 10–12 minutes or until the eggs are cooked through.

6. Season to taste with a little more salt and pepper, sprinkle over the chopped coriander and serve.

KAYA COCONUT JAM ON TOAST WITH BOILED EGGS AND TAMARI

SERVES 4

This is our take on a classic Singaporean breakfast dish. It sounds a bit wacky, but it's seriously amazing. The boiled eggs with tamari and white pepper are delicious on their own, even if you don't get around to making the coconut jam, but it's really straightforward and extremely delicious, like a Southeast Asian *dulce de leche*. It's pretty sweet, but it's beautifully counterpointed by the saltiness of the tamari in this dish.

For the coconut jam
140g/5oz/scant ¾ cup palm sugar
400ml (1 can) coconut milk
4 egg yolks
2 tsp cornflour

To serve
8 slices wholemeal bread (or your favourite bread)
about 50g/1¾oz/4 tbsp butter
4 eggs, boiled
2 tsp tamari
white pepper

1. To make the coconut jam, put the palm sugar in a heavy-bottomed saucepan over a low–medium heat and leave to melt, stirring occasionally. Once the sugar has melted, continue to heat until it caramelizes, stirring regularly until it is golden brown and you can smell the caramel. Very carefully pour in 300ml/10fl oz/1¼ cups of the coconut milk and continue to heat, whisking regularly until the mixture starts to thicken very slightly; this should take 5–10 minutes.

2. Meanwhile, put the egg yolks in a mixing bowl, add the remaining coconut milk and whisk until well combined.

3. Once the caramel and coconut mixture is ready, gently whisk about half of the mixture into the egg yolks (this prevents them from curdling) and then return it all to the pan. Place over a medium heat, whisking continuously until it becomes custard-like; this should take about 6–8 minutes. In a small bowl, mix the cornflour with 2 tsp water and stir that into the jam. Cook for a final couple of minutes, still stirring continuously. Strain through a sieve into a bowl and leave to cool to room temperature, then cover with clingfilm (plastic wrap) and place in the fridge until cold and set, ideally overnight.

4. When you're ready to eat, toast the bread and generously spread with butter. Top four slices with a liberal amount of kaya and make into sandwiches using the other four slices. Cut into halves.

5. Put the boiled eggs in a bowl and season with the tamari and a couple of pinches of white pepper and enjoy with the sandwiches.

SPELT PIKELETS WITH MASCARPONE AND CINNAMON SPICED APPLES

SERVES 2

Spelt has certainly become more popular in recent times but it's one of the most ancient of grains, even warranting a couple of mentions in the *Bible*. It contains a huge range of nutrients, needs little in the way of fertilizers and pesticides, and some find it easier to digest than common wheat (although it does contain gluten and so is not suitable for coeliacs). It's also delicious and has a sweet nutty flavour that's amplified in this recipe by the addition of ground almonds. While we love having these for breakfast, the indulgent cinnamon and apple topping makes them a real treat at any time of the day.

85g/3oz/scant ¾ cup spelt flour

85g/3oz/scant 1 cup ground almonds

¼ tsp baking powder

½ tsp vanilla extract

½ egg

15g/½oz/1 tbsp lightly salted butter, melted, plus a little extra to cook the pikelets

1½ tsp rapadura sugar or other unrefined brown sugar

225ml/8fl oz/scant 1 cup whole milk

For the spiced apples

45g/1½oz/3 tbsp lightly salted butter

½ tsp ground cinnamon

3 cinnamon sticks

½ tsp ground allspice

2 cooking apples, peeled, cut into wedges

60g/2oz/5 tbsp rapadura sugar or other unrefined brown sugar

To serve

125g/4½oz/½ cup mascarpone

2 sprigs mint

handful flaked (sliced) almonds, toasted

1. First, make the spiced apples: melt the butter in a pan or skillet, add the ground cinnamon, cinnamon sticks and allspice, then add the apples and sugar and mix thoroughly. Keep stirring, moving the apples about, for 5–10 minutes or until the apples are cooked through. Take off the heat and leave to one side.

2. To make the pikelet batter, put the spelt flour, ground almonds and the remaining ingredients together in a large bowl and mix thoroughly.

3. To cook the pikelets, melt a little butter in a frying pan or skillet and then add about 3 tablespoons of the batter. Turn the heat to low and wait until the pikelet begins to bubble around the sides. Gently lift up the edges and flip it over to cook the other side. When both sides are golden, transfer to a plate and repeat the process to make the rest of the pikelets.

4. To serve, place 3–4 pikelets in a stack on each plate. Top with a generous amount of the spiced apples and a good dollop of mascarpone. Garnish with a sprig of mint, one of the cinnamon sticks used to make the spiced apples and a few flaked almonds.

CHEDDAR CHEESE LATKES WITH APPLE, CRÈME FRAÎCHE AND CHIVES

SERVES 2

A mighty brunch number, this take on a traditional Jewish favourite is a great dish to enjoy on a lazy Sunday. We've used baking potatoes, but other potatoes are OK as long as they're starchy. The real key to the success of these latkes is to make sure the potatoes are as dried out as possible before you whisk in the eggs.

4 baking potatoes, peeled and grated

1 onion, finely chopped

½ tsp salt

2 eggs, lightly beaten

60g/2oz cheddar cheese, grated

30g/1oz/¾ cup fresh wholemeal breadcrumbs

4 tbsp olive oil

100g/3½oz/scant ½ cup crème fraîche

2 firm apples, thinly sliced

10 chives, finely chopped

1. Place the grated potato in a mixing bowl half filled with cold water. Leave to soak for a couple of minutes, then strain and return to the mixing bowl. Mix in the onion and salt and then transfer the mix back to the strainer and leave for about 15 minutes, squeezing it every now and then to make it as dry as possible. Tip the mixture onto a clean tea towel and then roll it into a sausage shape and wring out any last traces of liquid (you may need to do this in two batches) and again return it to a mixing bowl.

2. Add the eggs, cheese and breadcrumbs to the potato mixture and mix well.

3. Heat the olive oil in a skillet or frying pan. Add 2 tablespoons of the potato mixture per latke (we usually do two or three at a time), flatten it with a spoon so it's fairly thin and cook over a medium–low heat for about 5 minutes, until the underside is nicely coloured. Flip and cook the other side for about 5 minutes, or until golden brown. Remove from the skillet and place on a paper towel to drain. Repeat until you've used up all the mixture. If you like, you can keep the cooked latkes on a wire rack in the oven on a low heat to keep warm (place a roasting tray underneath to catch any oil that drips). If the mixture starts to seem too wet, add a few more breadcrumbs, and just add a touch more oil if the pan ever gets too dry..

4. Serve in a stack with a generous dollop of crème fraîche, a scattering of sliced apple and the chopped chives.

MILLET PORRIDGE WITH PRUNE COMPOTE AND FLAKED ALMONDS

SERVES 2
V / WF / GF

We weren't too sure about millet until we had the most wonderful experience of it at a farmstay in Karnataka in southwest India. All round, this was some of the best food (and company) we've ever enjoyed and this porridge was easy to translate into our regular cooking back home. In India they used buffalo milk, which made it amazingly creamy – it can be tracked down if you fancy having a go – but we've chosen to keep it vegan by using almond milk. If you're still not sold on millet you can also play around with quinoa or amaranth, two other super-nutritious grains. We've used wholegrain millet in this recipe but you could speed it up a bit by using millet flakes instead. If you use the flakes, just skip the part about blitzing the millet until it's like flour.

250g/9oz/1¼ cups wholegrain millet
375ml/13fl oz/1½ cups almond milk
375ml/13fl oz/1½ cups water
4 tbsp flaked (sliced) almonds, toasted

For the prune compote
250g/9oz/1½ cups soft, ready-to-eat prunes (or soak dried hard prunes overnight)
125ml/4fl oz/½ cup water
35g/1¼oz/2½ tbsp rapadura sugar or other unrefined brown sugar
2 cloves
½ cinnamon stick
grated zest of ½ orange, plus a little extra to garnish

1. To make the prune compote, put the prunes, water, sugar, cloves, cinnamon and orange zest in a pan over a low heat, cover with a lid and cook for 20–25 minutes, stirring occasionally.

2. Meanwhile, toast the millet in a hot dry pan for a couple of minutes or until it becomes quite fragrant. Transfer to a blender and blitz until flour-like.

3. Put the blitzed millet in a pan with the almond milk and water. Bring to the boil, stirring regularly, and then turn down the heat and simmer for a couple of minutes until it tastes cooked. If the porridge seems too thick, stir in a little hot water until it's the desired consistency.

4. Spoon into bowls and top with the prune compote, toasted almonds and a little orange zest.

SKYR WITH RYE BREAD SPRINKLE AND STEWED PEARS

We first discovered skyr in Iceland, whipped into the most fluffy, moreish butter we've ever eaten and swirled into a fabulous wild mushroom soup at Hotel Ranga, our base for a few exciting days in pursuit of the Northern lights. We next enjoyed skyr in Copenhagen, parfait style, on the rare breakfasts that didn't involve Danish pastries – or *snegls* (snails) as they're known there – and that was the inspiration for this dish. Skyr's loaded with health benefits: high in protein and probiotics but virtually fat free, and we were overjoyed to find it in UK supermarkets. No worries if you can't get hold of it: natural, Greek or plant-based yogurt will be delicious too.

Rye bread is another Nordic staple; it's high in fibre and provides a slow release of energy to keep your blood sugar steady. The rye sprinkle can be made in advance and stored in an airtight container for a couple of days. The pears are best made in advance and left overnight but they're also great when made and eaten on the same day. This recipe makes a generous amount of the pears but they'll keep well in the fridge if you don't eat them all in one go!

SERVES 2
VO

450g/1lb/1¾ cups skyr

For the stewed pears
100g/3½oz/½ cup rapadura sugar or other unrefined brown sugar
400ml/14fl oz/1 ⅔ cups water
pinch of saffron
4 pears, peeled, cored, and cut into quarters

For the rye bread sprinkle
2 slices rye bread, crumbled
1 tbsp ground almonds
1½ tbsp rapadura sugar or other unrefined brown sugar
½ tsp mixed spice
1 tbsp coconut oil

1. Begin by making the stewed pears. Put the sugar, water and saffron in a pan and bring to the boil. Add the pears and bring back to the boil, then turn down the heat, cover with a lid and simmer for about 15 minutes until the pears are just tender. Using a slotted spoon, remove the pears from the syrup and leave to one side, keeping the syrup. Leave to cool and then put the pears in a jar or bowl, add the syrup, cover and store in the fridge until you're ready to serve.

2. Meanwhile, make the rye sprinkle. Put all the ingredients except the coconut oil into a food processor and blitz to breadcrumbs. In a frying pan or skillet, melt the coconut oil over a high heat and then add the breadcrumbs, stirring constantly to prevent catching for about 3 minutes. Tip them into a bowl until ready to use. If making them in advance, leave to cool before transferring to an airtight container.

3. Spoon the skyr into bowls. Add the pears, drizzling over a little of the syrup, and top with the sprinkle.

Vegan option Use plant-based yogurt in place of skyr.

SUPER-HEALTHy BREAKFAST RUSKS

MAKES
ABOUT 22
RUSKS

A South African staple, these biscuits make a great on-the-go breakfast or a nutritious snack at any time of the day. They're epically good dunked into a hot cup of tea. Don't panic if they seem very crumbly, it's how they're meant to be. Just make like a South African *ouma* (grandma) and take any leftover crumbs out to the garden to feed the birds.

125g/4½oz/generous ½ cup unsalted butter

1 egg

75g/2¾oz/⅓ cup unrefined soft brown sugar

125ml/4fl oz/½ cup buttermilk

250g/9oz/2 cups wholemeal self-raising flour

½ tsp baking powder

pinch of salt

¼ tsp lemon juice

50g/1¾oz/⅔ cup porridge (rolled) oats

75g/2¾oz/2½ cups branflakes, well crushed

30g/1oz/¼ cup pecans, crushed

50g/1¾oz/scant ½ cup dried cranberries, roughly chopped

2 tbsp golden flaxseeds

2 tbsp sunflower seeds

1. Preheat the oven to 200°C/400°F/Gas 6 and line a 30-cm/12-inch loaf tin with greaseproof (waxed) paper.

2. Slowly melt the butter in a pan and leave to cool slightly. Meanwhile, in a large mixing bowl, whisk together the egg, sugar and buttermilk for a couple of minutes. Mix in the melted butter, then sift in the flour, baking powder and salt and gently mix. Add the lemon juice, oats, branflakes, pecans, cranberries, flaxseeds and sunflower seeds, mix thoroughly and transfer to the lined tin.

3. Place in the oven for 25 minutes and then turn the heat down to 180°C/350°F/Gas 4 and bake for a further 25 minutes. Turn the heat down to 150°C/300°F/Gas 2 and bake for a final 15 minutes.

4. Leave to cool in the tin before turning out. Using a serrated knife, cut lengthways along the middle of the loaf. Then cut each strip into 2.5cm/1in pieces to form the rusks.

5. Turn the oven back on to 75°C/150°F (the lowest setting) and line a baking sheet with greaseproof paper. Put the rusks on the baking sheet and return to the oven for about 2 hours to fully dry out. Remove from the oven, cover with a tea towel and leave to cool for about hour or so until they seem fully hardened. Store in an airtight container.

CHAPTER 2
SALADS

BRAZILIAN BIRIBANDO SALAD

SERVES 2,
OR 4 AS A SIDE
VO / WF / GF

We first enjoyed this on holiday in Trancoso, a sleepy yet deeply bohemian fishing village in Brazil, rediscovered in the 1970s by a motley group of hippies, wanderers and artists, nicknamed the *biribandos*, after whom this vibrant and colourful dish is named.

The original uses fresh young coconut, cut into strips, and if you happen to be in the tropics and able to get hold of some, it's very yummy, but dried coconut also does the job.

2 carrots, julienned
2 small beetroots, julienned
45g/1½oz/½ cup shredded or desiccated coconut
60g/2oz/scant ½ cup cashews, crushed
40 mint leaves (30 torn, 10 chopped)
6 sprigs parsley, chopped
1 garlic clove, crushed
100g/3½oz/scant ½ cup natural yogurt
salt and black pepper
juice of ½ lime
1 tbsp black sesame seeds

1. Place the carrots, beetroots, coconut, cashews and torn mint in a large mixing bowl.

2. In another bowl, make the dressing by mixing together the parsley, chopped mint, garlic, yogurt, salt and pepper. Stir in the lime juice and then pour the dressing over the salad and mix through. Garnish with the black sesame seeds.

Vegan option Use a plant-based yogurt.

HONEY-ROASTED CARROT SALAD WITH BULGUR WHEAT, WALNUTS, POMEGRANATE SEEDS AND LABNEH

SERVES 2
VO

Heirloom carrots are a beauty to behold, especially if you can get them in different colours. But ordinary carrots are also delicious in this recipe.

Labneh is a favourite ingredient of ours, a strained yogurt widely used in eastern Mediterranean cuisine (see page 120). Super thick and with a bold tang, it's well worth hunting down, but if you struggle to find it, natural yogurt also works well.

500g/1lb 2oz heirloom carrots, cut in half lengthways (if using regular carrots cut into finger-length batons)

2 tbsp olive oil

2 sprigs thyme, leaves plucked

salt and black pepper

4 tsp runny honey

125g/4½oz/¾ cup bulgur wheat, cooked and cooled

2 tbsp chopped parsley

2 tbsp chopped mint

2 tsp lemon juice

3 tbsp labneh (see page 120)

50g/1¾oz/6 tbsp walnuts, toasted

seeds from ½ pomegranate

1. Preheat the oven to 200°C/400°F/Gas 6. Line a roasting tray with greaseproof (waxed) paper.

2. Put the carrots in a mixing bowl, add 4 teaspoons of the olive oil, the thyme leaves and a pinch of salt and pepper and mix well. Transfer to the lined roasting tray and roast for about 40 minutes, turning them around occasionally until they've started to take on some colour. Drizzle over the honey and roast for a further 10 minutes or so.

3. Meanwhile, place the cooked bulgur in a mixing bowl and combine with the parsley and mint, the remaining 2 teaspoons of olive oil, the lemon juice and a touch of salt and pepper.

4. Place the bulgur mix in a serving bowl and top with the carrots, labneh, walnuts and pomegranate seeds.

Vegan option Use agave in place of honey and a plant-based yogurt in place of labneh.

SEAWEED, WILD RICE, TOFU, SESAME AND SPRING ONION SALAD

SERVES 2,
OR 4 AS A SIDE
VO / WF / GF

This is a moody-looking salad; we're in love with the deep greens and purples of the sea vegetables. Seaweeds are so good for you, too, being rich in iodine, as well as all manner of antioxidants and a broad spectrum of vitamins.

Placing the spring onions in icy cold water is a little trick that makes them curl.

8g/¼oz dried sea vegetable salad (or dulse), soaked in cold water for about 10 minutes

3 spring onions (scallions), sliced lengthways and placed in icy cold water

200g/7oz/1¼ cups wild rice, cooked and cooled

200g/7oz fresh firm tofu, cut into bite-sized cubes

2 tbsp sesame seeds, to garnish

For the dressing

2 tbsp brown rice vinegar

1 tbsp tamari

2 tsp runny honey

½ tsp toasted sesame oil

15g/½oz fresh root ginger, finely chopped

1. Begin by making the dressing. Mix the vinegar, tamari, honey, sesame oil and ginger together in a bowl. Place to one side.

2. Drain the seaweed and spring onions and place in a large mixing bowl. Add the cooked rice and tofu. Mix well, then pour over the dressing and top with the sesame seeds.

Vegan option Use agave in place of honey.

FATTOUSH SALAD

SERVES 2
V

The original chopped salad: sometimes simple really is best and this quick and easy fattoush is one of our favourites for a light lunch or side dish. It's packed to the rafters with all the colours, flavours and vibrancy of the Middle East. Delicious on its own, it's also brilliant served with falafels, houmous, baba ganoush, pickles and flatbreads. Sumac is a wonderful spice made from bright red berries, with a fresh lemony taste. It's available in larger supermarkets as well as all Middle Eastern stores.

1 large wholewheat pita bread, toasted until crisp, broken into pieces

1 tbsp extra virgin olive oil

salt and black pepper

1 cucumber, cut into chunks

1 romaine lettuce, cut into strips about 1–2cm/¾in wide

10 cherry tomatoes, quartered

3 spring onions (scallions), green part only, finely sliced

½ bunch mint, leaves picked

1 small bunch flat-leaf parsley, leaves picked

For the dressing
4 tsp ground sumac
4 tsp warm water
2 garlic cloves, finely chopped
2 tsp white wine vinegar
juice of 1 lemon
125ml/4fl oz/½ cup extra virgin olive oil

1. First, make the dressing. In a small bowl, mix the sumac with the warm water and leave to soak for 15 minutes. Once soaked, in a larger bowl whisk together the garlic, vinegar, soaked sumac and lemon juice and then slowly trickle in the olive oil, whisking continuously until it begins to emulsify. Add a couple of pinches of salt and whisk in before setting the dressing to one side.

2. For the salad, place the pita pieces in a small bowl, drizzle the olive oil over them and season with salt and pepper. In a large bowl, gently toss together the cucumber, lettuce, tomatoes, spring onions, mint, parsley and pita pieces. Add half of the dressing and mix through. Add more dressing to taste and it's ready to serve.

SPELT GRAIN SALAD WITH ROASTED AUBERGINE, CHERRY TOMATOES AND GOAT'S CHEESE

SERVES 2, OR 4 AS A SIDE

We could wax lyrical endlessly about how much we love spelt. We use it a lot in our day-to-day cooking but generally we've always gone for the pearled version. Admittedly the pearls do take less time to cook, but we've just discovered how truly delicious wholegrain spelt is (and this is a wholefood book after all); an amplified version of all the nutty, grainy chewiness of the pearl and with all its fibre and micronutrients kept in. It's worth the extra 30 minutes of cooking time.

250g/9oz/1¼ cups spelt grains
1 large aubergine (eggplant), cut into small cubes
1 tbsp salt
3 tbsp olive oil
10 cherry tomatoes, halved
½ red onion, finely sliced
1 small bunch mint, leaves plucked and chopped
1 small bunch flat-leaf parsley, plucked
100g/3½oz goat's cheese, crumbled
salt and black pepper, to taste

For the dressing
juice of ½ lemon
2 tsp honey
4 tsp olive oil

1. Bring a pan of water to the boil, add the spelt grains, cover with a lid and simmer for about 50 minutes or until tender. Drain and place to one side.

2. Meanwhile, preheat the oven to 200°C/400°F/Gas 6. Line a roasting tray with greaseproof (waxed) paper.

3. Put the aubergine in a large bowl, add the salt, mix thoroughly and leave to one side for about 10 minutes. Place in a colander, rinse off the salt and drain the aubergine of any excess water before returning it to the bowl and pouring over the olive oil. Mix well and then transfer to the lined roasting tray and roast for about 45 minutes, turning after 20–25 minutes, until the aubergine cubes look nicely roasted. Leave to cool.

4. To make the dressing, in a bowl, mix the lemon juice, honey and olive oil.

5. In a serving bowl, combine the cooked spelt, roasted aubergine, cherry tomatoes, red onion, mint, parsley and goat's cheese. Pour over the dressing, mix gently and season to taste with salt and pepper.

SWEET POTATO, RYE GRAIN, TARRAGON AND RICOTTA SALAD

**SERVES 2
VO**

150g/5½oz/¾ cup rye grains, soaked overnight

salt and black pepper

600g/1lb 5oz sweet potatoes, peeled and cut into chunks

300g/10½oz butternut squash, peeled and cut into chunks

1½ tbsp olive oil

6 sprigs tarragon, leaves plucked

125g/4½oz/½ cup ricotta

For the dressing

2 tsp lemon juice

2 tsp Dijon mustard

2 tsp honey

2 tsp olive oil

Just to be clear, rye grains really do need to be soaked properly. There's no getting around it and so this isn't a spur-of-the-moment salad, although you could use spelt grains or short-grain brown rice if you don't have the time to leave the rye overnight. But rye is an ingredient well worth getting to know: its flavour is deep and complex and it's super-healthy, being very high in fibre and magnesium as well as many other nutrients. Rye is beloved in Nordic cultures and we've kept with a Nordic vibe, pairing it with the delicious herb tarragon.

1. Preheat the oven to 200°C/400°F/Gas 6.

2. Bring a pan of water to the boil. Drain and rinse the rye grains before adding them to the boiling water, along with a pinch of salt. You don't need to be too precise about how much water, but it should be in the region of four parts water to one part rye. Cover with a lid and bring back to the boil, then turn the heat down to medium and simmer for 50–60 minutes or until the rye grains are tender (they will still have a little bite). Drain and place to one side to cool.

3. Meanwhile, put the sweet potato and butternut squash into a mixing bowl, add the olive oil and a generous pinch of salt and pepper and mix well. Transfer to a roasting tray lined with greaseproof (waxed) paper and and roast for 50–60 minutes, stirring occasionally, until the sweet potatoes and squash have taken on good colour and taste cooked. Once ready, set aside to cool.

4. While they're roasting and the rye is still cooking, make the dressing. Combine the lemon juice, mustard, honey, olive oil and a little salt and pepper in a bowl and place to one side.

5. Once everything is cooled, gently combine the rye, sweet potato mix, tarragon leaves and dressing in a large bowl. Spoon in the ricotta and serve, adding a little more black pepper if you like.

Vegan option Leave out the ricotta and use agave instead of honey.

WARM ROASTED BEETROOT SALAD WITH CRÈME FRAÎCHE, THYME AND HAZELNUTS

Beetroot is one of our favourite vegetables – full of vitamins and minerals, packed with antioxidants and oh so pretty, we just can't get enough of it and this is a real winner of a combination. It's straight-up delicious.

The technique of roasting whole cloves of garlic along with other vegetables is one we often use. You don't have to eat the garlic cloves (although we often do) but their presence in the roasting tray infuses a gentle garlic flavour to whatever else is in there.

SERVES 2
AS A SIDE
WF / GF

700g/1lb 9oz uncooked beetroots, peeled and cut into wedges
3 tbsp olive oil, plus extra to drizzle
6 sprigs thyme, plus extra to garnish
3 garlic cloves, skin left on
½ tsp salt
black pepper
2 generous tbsp crème fraîche
20g/¾oz/3 tbsp hazelnuts, roasted and crushed

1. Preheat the oven to 180°C/350°F/Gas 4. Line a roasting tray with greaseproof (waxed) paper.

2. In a bowl, mix the beetroot wedges with the olive oil, thyme, garlic, salt and a little cracked black pepper. Mix well and then transfer to the lined roasting tray and roast for 1¼–1½ hours until the beetroot is well roasted, stirring occasionally.

3. Leaving the garlic cloves in the roasting tray, pile the beetroot wedges on a serving plate and garnish with the crème fraîche, hazelnuts and thyme. Best eaten while still warm.

WHOLEGRAIN GLASS NOODLE SALAD WITH SMOKED TOFU AND MIXED SPROUTS

SERVES 2
V / WF / GF

Loaded with all the colours, flavours and vibrancy of Southeast Asia, this is a quick and easy salad, ideal for a light lunch or dinner. Many large supermarkets and Asian groceries now stock wholegrain rice vermicelli (also more poetically known as glass noodles) but they're also easily bought online if you're struggling to find them. Smoked tofu, mixed sprouts and seeds are ingredients that we use all the time to make sure our dishes have plenty of protein.

125g/4½oz dried wholegrain rice vermicelli

1 carrot, cut into thin strips

100g/3½oz mangetout (snow peas), cut into thin strips

30g/1oz coriander (cilantro), chopped

150g/5½oz mixed sprouts (eg mungbean, chickpea, lentil)

100g/3½oz smoked tofu, thinly sliced

1 tbsp sesame seeds, lightly toasted

For the dressing

2 garlic cloves, finely chopped

45g/1½oz fresh root ginger, finely chopped

1 red chilli, deseeded and finely chopped

3 tbsp unrefined brown sugar

juice of 4 limes

2 tsp tamari

1. Put the noodles in a bowl, pour boiling water over them and leave to soak for 4 minutes. Drain in a sieve and then run cold water over the noodles until they have cooled down. Drain well and leave to one side.

2. To make the dressing, in a pestle and mortar, crush together the garlic, ginger, chilli and sugar until they form a paste. Add the lime juice and tamari and stir.

3. Put the carrot, mangetout, coriander, sprouts, smoked tofu and noodles in a large bowl and gently mix together by hand, then pour over the dressing and continue to mix by hand until the dressing is well incorporated. Sprinkle over the sesame seeds and serve.

CHAPTER 3
SOUPS AND
STEWS

SWEET POTATO AND COCONUT SOUP WITH TOASTED PUMPKIN SEEDS

SERVES 4
V / WF / GF

The soothing creamy sweetness of sweet potato and coconut combined with cinnamon makes this a truly warming soup for a cold evening. Grab some bread, get yourself comfy on the sofa and you'll feel better in no time.

4 tsp coconut oil

1 onion, chopped

1 garlic clove, crushed

20g/¾oz fresh root ginger, chopped

½ tsp ground cinnamon

700g/1lb 9oz sweet potatoes, peeled and roughly chopped

2 carrots, roughly chopped

salt and black pepper

500ml/18fl oz/2 cups vegetable stock

500ml/18fl oz/2 cups water

400ml (1 can) coconut milk

50g/1¾oz/6 tbsp pumpkin seeds, toasted

1. Melt the coconut oil in a Dutch oven or large pan, add the onion and sauté for a couple of minutes until translucent. Add the garlic and ginger and cook for a couple of minutes. Stir in the cinnamon, then add the sweet potatoes and carrots and a pinch of salt and pepper and cook for a minute or so, stirring regularly. Pour in the stock and water, cover with a lid and bring to the boil, then turn the heat down to medium and simmer for 20 minutes or until the potatoes and carrots are soft.

2. Stir in the coconut milk and bring to the boil before removing from the heat. Using a stick blender – or carefully transferring the soup to a blender (we usually do it in two batches to be safer) – blend until smooth.

3. Serve in bowls, with toasted pumpkin seeds sprinkled on top.

CANNELLINI BEAN, FENNEL AND SEAWEED BOUILLABAISSE WITH GARLIC AND SAFFRON ROUILLE

Inspired by the Provençal classic, this is a vegan version of a dish that immediately conjures up images of lazy sunny afternoons and splashing about in the sea in the south of France. As we're not using fish, we've given it a connection to the sea by using sea vegetable salad; you could use dried nori seaweed to get the same effect, but the nori doesn't need to be soaked, it can just be shredded and added in at the end.

The garlicky rouille is the icing on the cake and is a handy recipe in itself if you're ever looking for something delicious to go with bread. We just wouldn't recommend it if you're about to go on a date!

pinch of saffron

250ml/9fl oz/1 cup white wine

2 tbsp olive oil

1 onion, chopped

1 stick celery, chopped

2 garlic cloves, crushed

1 tsp tomato purée (tomato paste)

1 fennel bulb, roughly chopped

1 red pepper, roughly chopped

1 bay leaf

2 plum tomatoes

5 sprigs thyme, leaves plucked

500ml/18fl oz/2 cups vegetable stock

400g (1 can) cannellini beans

5g dried sea vegetable salad, soaked in cold water for about 10 minutes

1 tbsp chopped parsley

1 lemon, cut into quarters

1 wholewheat sourdough loaf, sliced and toasted, to serve

For the rouille

pinch of saffron

2 tsp white wine

4 egg yolks

1 garlic clove, crushed

1½ tsp smoked paprika

1 red chilli, deseeded and finely chopped

3 tbsp lemon juice

salt and black pepper

300ml/10fl oz/1¼ cups olive oil

1. Begin by making the bouillabaisse. Place the saffron in the white wine and leave to soak. Put the olive oil, onion, celery and garlic in a large pan or Dutch oven over a medium heat and sauté for about 5 minutes, stirring occasionally. Stir in the tomato purée, fennel and red pepper and continue to sauté for a couple of minutes. Pour in the wine and saffron, add the bay leaf and simmer for 3–5 minutes. Add the tomatoes and thyme leaves and pour in the vegetable stock. Stir, then cover with a lid and simmer for about 30 minutes, stirring occasionally.

2. Meanwhile, make the rouille. Soak the saffron in the wine for a couple of minutes. Put the egg yolks in a mixing bowl, add the garlic, paprika, chilli, lemon juice, saffron and wine, and a pinch of salt and pepper and whisk vigorously for a couple of minutes. Then slowly drizzle in the olive oil a little at a time, whisking continuously with the other hand until the oil is fully incorporated. This does take a bit of time so brace yourself for a little arm workout! Whisk in 2 teaspoons of warm water and place to one side.

3. Back at the bouillabaisse, stir in the cannellini beans and seaweed and gently bring to the boil. Turn off the heat and add the parsley and salt and pepper to taste. Serve immediately in bowls. Squeeze a lemon wedge over each one and enjoy with toasted sourdough smothered with, or dipped in, rouille.

KHICHDI

Khichdi, or *khichri*, is a cornerstone of Ayurvedic nutritional healing. There are endless variations and you can experiment with additional herbs, spices or vegetables depending on what feels good to you. They're relatively simple stews and are a key food in *panchakarma* (detoxifying and revitalizing) cures because they are so easily digested.

Ghee is a fantastic ingredient, a type of clarified butter that originated in India and is widely used in south Asian cookery. Ayurveda has long revered ghee as being the best fat you can consume and has recognized its many health benefits, not least that it contains high levels of antioxidants and beneficial omega 3 and 9 fatty acids. It's used in India as much in devotional rituals as it is in cookery.

Yellow split peas and the more traditionally used mung dal are not quite the same thing (mung dal are a little smaller), but just use whichever one you can find.

SERVES 4
VO / WF / GF

1 tbsp ghee

½ onion, chopped

2 garlic cloves, crushed

15g/½oz fresh root ginger, finely chopped

2 carrots, chopped

1 tsp turmeric

1½ tsp ground cumin

½ tsp ground cinnamon

15 curry leaves

150g/5½oz/¾ cup yellow split peas (or mung dal)

200g/7oz/generous 1 cup wholegrain basmati rice

salt and black pepper

1.8 litres/3 pints/7 cups water

4 tsp tamari

10g/⅓oz coriander (cilantro), torn

1. Melt the ghee in a large pan over a medium heat, add the onion and sauté for a couple of minutes. Add the garlic and ginger and cook for a couple of minutes, stirring occasionally. Add the carrots, turmeric, cumin, cinnamon and curry leaves and cook for a minute or so before adding the split peas, rice, a pinch of salt and the water. Cover with a lid, bring to the boil and then turn down the heat and simmer for 60–75 minutes, stirring occasionally, until the split peas and rice are fully cooked and it's become a bit mushy.

2. Stir in the tamari and a little salt and black pepper to taste. Top with coriander and serve.

Vegan option Use coconut oil in place of ghee.

BROWN RICE MULLIGATAWNY

SERVES 2–4
V / WF / GF

A winning Anglo–Indian number, mulligatawny is one of our top feel-better-quickly soups – although perhaps it should really be called a stew, since it's so hearty. It's an ideal thing to knock up in a cast-iron Dutch oven if you have one.

1 tbsp coconut oil
1 onion, chopped
10g/⅓oz fresh root ginger, chopped
1 stick celery, chopped
2 garlic cloves, crushed
2 tsp mild curry powder
1 carrot, diced
500ml/18fl oz/2 cups vegetable stock
400g (1 can) chopped tomatoes
10 curry leaves
5 sprigs thyme, chopped
2 apples, peeled, cored and diced
½ tsp chopped fresh red chilli
salt and black pepper
100g/3½oz/½ cup short-grain brown rice, cooked
200ml/7fl oz/¾ cup coconut milk
10g/⅓oz coriander (cilantro), chopped

1. Melt the coconut oil in a Dutch oven or large pan, add the onion and ginger and sauté for a couple of minutes. Add the celery, garlic and curry powder, turn the heat down to low and cook for a couple of minutes, stirring regularly. Add the carrot and cook, stirring occasionally, for another couple of minutes before pouring in the stock and tomatoes and adding the curry leaves, thyme, apples, chilli and a pinch of salt and pepper. Bring to the boil and then turn the heat down, cover with a lid and simmer for about 30 minutes (this is a good time to cook the rice if you haven't already).

2. Add the rice, stir, and then bring the soup back to the boil before stirring in the coconut milk and coriander. Simmer for a couple of minutes, season to taste and serve hot.

PHO WITH PAK CHOI, EDAMAME AND BROWN RICE NOODLES

We absolutely love *pho* but it can be hard to find a Vietnamese restaurant that doesn't put fish sauce in it; luckily it's easy to make at home. Brown rice noodles are a favourite ingredient of ours and are available in many supermarkets and in health food shops. We particularly like the King Soba Noodle Culture brand. Edamame beans are a handy snack to keep in the freezer and they're also a super protein boost for vegan meals.

SERVES 4
V / WF / GF

2 cinnamon sticks

3 star anise

3 cloves

3 carrots, roughly chopped

1 onion, roughly chopped

10g/⅓oz fresh root ginger, roughly chopped

125g/4½oz fresh shitake mushrooms, cut in half, stems removed and kept to one side

2 pak choi, cut into 2.5cm/1in pieces, stalks removed and kept to one side

2 garlic cloves, crushed

2 litres/3½ pints/2 quarts vegetable stock

salt and black pepper

250g/9oz frozen edamame beans in pods

16 cherry tomatoes, halved

4 spring onions (scallions), roughly chopped

1 red chilli, thinly sliced, plus a little extra to serve

24 Thai basil leaves, plus a little extra to serve

24 mint leaves, plus a little extra to serve

12 sprigs coriander (cilantro), plus a little extra to serve

125g/4½oz beansprouts

2 tbsp tamari

250g/9oz brown rice noodles, cooked according to packet instructions

2 limes, halved

1. Put the cinnamon, star anise, cloves, carrots, onion, ginger, mushroom stems, pak choi stalks, garlic and stock in a Dutch oven or large pan, cover with a lid and bring to the boil. Turn the heat down and simmer for 15–20 minutes.

2. Meanwhile, bring a pot of water to the boil, add a pinch of salt and then add the edamame and blanch for 5 minutes. Drain and run under cold water to refresh. Remove the beans from the pods and place in a mixing bowl. Add the cherry tomatoes, spring onions, red chilli, Thai basil, mint, coriander and beansprouts and place to one side.

3. Once the broth is ready, strain and then return it to the pan and bring it back to the boil. Add the shitake and cook over a high heat for a minute or so, then add the pak choi and tamari and cook for a further 2 minutes. Add the contents of the mixing bowl and cook for a couple of minutes before adding the noodles. Taste and add a little more tamari if you like. It's easiest to serve if you use tongs to place some of the noodles and vegetables into each bowl and then use a ladle for the broth. Add a little more chilli, Thai basil, mint and coriander to each bowl according to personal preference. Garnish with half a lime and a little black pepper.

RED LENTIL, BUCKWHEAT, KALE AND CHERRY TOMATO SOUP

SERVES 4
V / WF / GF

This is a hearty soup, one of those really soothing bowls of food that pick you up on off days or when the sky's been grey for too long. Buckwheat is rich in protein and – despite its name – is not related to regular wheat, so it is a great option for anyone looking to avoid wheat or gluten. We were served it countless times on a winter trip to Siberia – and anything that helps the Russians survive their long hard winters must be a nutritional powerhouse.

100g/3½oz/⅔ cup roasted buckwheat (kasha)
100g/3½oz/½ cup red lentils
2 tbsp olive oil
1 large onion, chopped
2 sticks celery, chopped
salt and black pepper
1 red pepper, chopped
2 garlic cloves, crushed
1 tsp dried thyme
2 bay leaves
10 cherry tomatoes, halved
1 litre/1¾ pints/4 cups vegetable stock
100g/3½oz kale, torn
1 small bunch parsley, chopped
1 tsp apple cider vinegar
1 tbsp tamari

1. Mix together the buckwheat and lentils and rinse thoroughly with cold water. Drain, then put them in a pan and fill the pan with water. Bring to the boil over a high heat and then turn the heat down and simmer until they're soft; this should take about 15 minutes. Drain and place to one side.

2. Meanwhile, heat the olive oil in a pan, add the onion and celery and a little salt and pepper and sauté over a high heat until they start taking on some colour. Add the red pepper and garlic and cook, stirring occasionally, for about 2 minutes. Add the thyme and cook, stirring occasionally, for about 5 minutes or until it has all taken on some colour.

3. Add the bay leaves and cherry tomatoes, turn the heat down to medium and cook for about 3 minutes until the tomatoes have started to break up. Add the stock, cover with a lid and turn the heat back up to high, continuing to stir regularly until it comes to the boil. Turn the heat back down to a simmer for a couple of minutes, then add the lentil and buckwheat mix and cook for a further 5 minutes.

4. Add the kale, parsley, vinegar and tamari and cook for a final 5 minutes. Serve hot.

SHITAKE MISO BROTH WITH TOFU AND SHIRATAKI NOODLES

Widely enjoyed since forever in Japan, shirataki are jelly-like noodles made from the konjac yam – they have recently become all the rage in the West. They're a wheat-free and gluten-free alternative to traditional noodles and are also naturally low carb, low fat and low in calories. We use the Yutaka brand's brown shirataki noodles, which are soft and ready to use after a quick rinse. They're sold in health food shops, Japanese food shops or online but don't worry if you can't find them, or fancy changing it up a bit: buckwheat noodles are also great in this recipe – cook them according to the packet instructions before using in the same way as the shirataki. Miso paste is another brilliant ingredient. It's a great way to add that elusive umami and, being fermented, it's also a fab way to get some extra probiotic goodness.

SERVES 2–4
V / WF

2 litres/3½ pints/2 quarts water

2 tbsp tamari

85g/3oz fresh shitake mushrooms, stems removed and kept to one side

3 spring onions (scallions), sliced

15g/½oz dried wakame

170g (1 pack) brown shirataki noodles, rinsed

200g/7oz firm fresh tofu, cut into cubes

5 stems cavolo nero (or kale), stems removed, leaves chopped

45g/1½oz/3 tbsp brown rice miso paste

white pepper

1. Begin by making a stock. Put the water in a large pan, add 1 tablespoon of the tamari, the mushrooms including the stems, one of the spring onions and a third of the wakame. Cover and bring to the boil, then reduce the heat and simmer for 10–15 minutes.

2. Meanwhile, soak the remaining wakame in cold water for about 5 minutes or until rehydrated. Drain the shirataki noodles and place to one side.

3. In a large mixing bowl, put the remaining spring onions, the tofu cubes, the cavolo nero, the noodles and the soaked wakame. Leave to one side.

4. When it's ready, strain the stock into another pan. Remove the shitake mushrooms from the strainer (but not the stalks), leave to cool slightly, then slice and add to the mixing bowl.

5. Reheat the stock over a medium heat and whisk in the miso paste. Add the remaining tamari and then turn the heat up and pour in the contents of the mixing bowl. Cook for a couple of minutes, stirring occasionally, and then serve immediately. Garnish with a pinch of white pepper.

CHAPTER 4
MAINS

BUDDHA BOWL

SERVES 4
V (WITHOUT HALLOUMI)
WF / GF

Now what exactly *is* a Buddha bowl? We first heard the term coined by an American chef friend of ours and thought it was a very cool concept that we interpreted as a healthy bowl of your favourite stuff. It was on this premise that we devised our signature Buddha Bowls, which fast became the lynchpin of our street food business, and for the past six years we've dished up thousands of them at markets, festivals and events up and down the country.

Every bowl contains Massaman-style curry with new potatoes, pineapple and soya chunks, carrot and kimchi pickle, flash-steamed seasonal greens, omega seed sprinkle and short-grain brown rice; grilled halloumi is optional. While the whole shebang takes quite a lot of work, it's well worth it if you've got time – remember that the kimchi needs to be made at least a week or two in advance. The curry paste can also be made in advance and kept in a sealed container in the fridge for up to 3 days. Alternatively, you can use a shop-bought Massaman paste or kimchi (or both) to speed it up. Just make sure they're veggie, as they often have fish sauce or shrimp paste lurking in them. We hope you enjoy it – come and see us at our van if you ever fancy an original!

For the Massaman-style paste

2 cloves

1 tbsp coriander seeds

6 black peppercorns

½ cinnamon stick

4 green cardamom pods, seeds only

1 tsp cumin seeds

¼ tsp freshly grated nutmeg

1 tbsp vegetable oil

2 sticks lemongrass, chopped

5 garlic cloves, crushed

2 tbsp chopped galangal

5 dried red chillies, deseeded

2 tbsp chopped coriander (cilantro)

100g/3½oz shallots, roughly chopped

Ingredients continue overleaf >>

1. To make the curry paste, put the cloves, coriander seeds, peppercorns, cinnamon, cardamom seeds and cumin in a hot dry wok and lightly toast for a couple of minutes or so. Transfer to a coffee grinder or pestle and mortar and grind to a powder. Add the nutmeg.

2. Heat the vegetable oil in the wok, then add the lemongrass, garlic, galangal, dried chillies, coriander and shallots. Sauté for about 10 minutes over a high heat until the mixture starts to turn golden, adding a splash of water if it gets too dry. Transfer to a blender, add the spice mix and 4 tablespoons of water and blend to a smooth paste.

3. When you're ready to get the curry going, gently melt the coconut oil in a pan, add the curry paste and cook for a minute or so, stirring regularly, then add the palm sugar and cook for a further 5 minutes. Pour in the coconut milk, add the tamari and star anise and bring to the boil, then reduce the heat and simmer for about 10 minutes, stirring occasionally.   Method continues overleaf >>

For the curry

1 tbsp coconut oil

20g/¾oz/1½ tbsp palm sugar

800ml (2 cans) coconut milk

2 tbsp tamari

2 star anise

400g/14oz new potatoes, boiled and cut into chunks

400g/14oz canned pineapple chunks in juice

75g/2½oz soya chunks, soaked in hot water until soft, drained

To serve

short-grain brown rice, cooked

1 batch carrot and kimchi pickle (page 109)

1 batch flash-steamed seasonal greens (page 113)

4 tbsp omega seeds (we use a mix of golden flaxseeds, brown flaxseeds, poppy seeds, sunflower seeds and sesame seeds)

225g/8oz halloumi, cut into 8 slices and grilled (optional)

Strain and then return to the pan along with the potatoes, pineapple (including the juice) and soya chunks. Bring to the boil and then reduce the heat and simmer for a couple of minutes.

4. Serve over brown rice and top with a generous spoonful of carrot and kimchi pickle, a whack of flash-steamed greens, a tablespoon of omega seeds and two slices each of grilled halloumi, if using.

BIBIMBAP BOWL

SERVES 2
VO

This is not a traditional *bibimbap* but it is a glorious bowl of food inspired by that signature Korean dish, which translates as 'mixed rice'. For ease, we've suggested shop-bought gochujang (fermented chilli pepper paste); there are several brands available, in supermarkets and Asian grocers, but make sure you choose one without fish products. Similarly, there are great vegetarian kimchis out there in health food shops, if you don't want to make your own.

4 tsp olive oil, plus extra for greasing

50g/1¾oz/3 tbsp brown rice miso paste

200g/7oz fresh firm tofu, cut into 8 slices

100g/3½oz fresh shitake mushrooms, stems removed, cut into thick slices

4 tsp tamari

½ cucumber, thinly sliced (ideally on a mandolin)

salt and black pepper

1½ tbsp brown rice vinegar

1 tsp mirin

150g/5½oz carrots, julienned

handful beansprouts

dash sesame oil

125g/4½oz baby spinach

2 eggs

250g/9oz/1¼ cups short-grain brown rice, cooked

100g/3½oz kimchi (optional, page 106)

30g/1oz/2 tbsp gochujang paste (shop-bought, but if you want to make your own, see page 121)

2 tsp black sesame seeds

5 spring onions (scallions), green parts only, very finely sliced

Vegan Option

This is just as yummy without eggs

1. Preheat the oven to 200°C/400°F/Gas 6. Line a roasting tray with greaseproof (waxed) paper smeared with a dash of olive oil.

2. Put the miso paste in a bowl along with 1 tablespoon water and mix. Add the tofu slices and mix until they're well coated. Transfer to the lined roasting tray and bake for 15 minutes, then flip the slices over and bake for a further 10 minutes. Remove from the oven and place to one side.

3. Meanwhile, put the mushrooms in a bowl with the tamari and olive oil and massage until the mushrooms are well coated. Place to one side.

4. Put the cucumber in another bowl and add a pinch of salt, the rice vinegar and mirin and leave to one side.

5. Place a wok over a high heat; when it's hot, add the mushrooms and cook for a minute or so, then add the carrots and stir-fry for about a minute. Add the beansprouts and a little black pepper and continue to stir-fry for another 2 minutes. Add a dash of sesame oil, taste, and add a dash more tamari if needed. Transfer to a bowl and place to one side.

6. Using the same wok, throw in the spinach and a generous pinch of salt and pepper, cook until wilted, and then tip the spinach into a colander.

7. Fry the eggs and then, when the tofu is baked, you're ready to assemble. Place the rice in the middle of each bowl. Around the sides, place the mushroom mix, wilted spinach, baked tofu, cucumber, kimchi, if using, and a large dollop of gochujang. Top with a fried egg, sesame seeds and spring onion greens.

ETHIOPIAN KIK ALICHA (SPLIT PEA STEW) WITH ATAKILT WAT (SPICED CABBAGE), CUCUMBER SALAD AND INJERA FLATBREAD

We've recently started experimenting with Ethiopian-inspired food after a couple of amazing meals at the Queen of Sheba in Kentish Town, London, and after discovering teff. Teff is a wonder ingredient and a staple of Ethiopian cuisine, used in grain form (added to soups, stews and salads) and also as flour, which is used to make the lynchpin of Ethiopian food, the *injera* bread; it's more than a bread (and gluten-free at that), it's also an eating utensil as all the stews and other dishes are served on the *injera* and it's then used to scoop them up.

Now we're going to come clean and admit that this is a bit of a cheat recipe. Traditionally *injera* is fermented for at least a few days, and if you do it that way you get a deeper flavour and all the benefits of fermentation, so it's definitely worth doing, if you're able to plan ahead; but for ease, we've gone with a speeded-up version, which means you can enjoy it the same day.

SERVES 2
VO / WF / GF

For the *injera* flatbreads
115g/4oz/1 cup teff flour
¼ tsp unrefined brown sugar
¾ tsp easy bake yeast
125ml/4fl oz/½ cup warm water
pinch of salt
1 tsp brown rice vinegar
¼ tsp baking powder
1 tsp olive oil

For the *kik alicha*
2 tbsp olive oil
1 onion, chopped
3 garlic cloves, crushed
10g/⅓oz fresh root ginger, chopped
½ tsp turmeric
Ingredients continue overleaf >>

1. Begin by starting off the *injera* flatbreads, put the teff flour, sugar, yeast and water in a large bowl and either whisk or mix thoroughly with your hands. Cover with a tea towel and leave to one side (ideally in a warm place) for at least an hour.

2. Meanwhile, prepare the *kik alicha*. Heat the olive oil in a Dutch oven or large pan, add the onion and sauté over a high heat for a couple of minutes. Add the garlic and ginger, turn the heat down to low and continue to cook for a couple of minutes. Add the turmeric and a pinch of salt and pepper and cook for another couple of minutes, stirring regularly. Pour in the stock, add the split peas, cover with a lid and turn the heat back up to bring it to the boil. Cook over a high heat for 20 minutes, stirring occasionally. Turn the heat down to low and cook for a further 40 minutes. Taste and season with more salt and pepper if you like.

Method continues overleaf >>

salt and black pepper
1 litre/1¾ pints/4 cups vegetable stock
200g/7oz/1 cup yellow split peas

For the *atakilt wat*
2 tbsp olive oil
1 onion, sliced
2 garlic cloves, crushed
2 carrots, diced
¼ tsp ground cumin
¼ tsp turmeric
½ head small white cabbage, stalk
removed, shredded
6 new potatoes, cut into bite-sized cubes
100ml/3½fl oz/scant ½ cup water

For the cucumber and yogurt salad
½ cucumber, finely sliced
100g/3½oz/scant ½ cup natural yogurt
¼ red onion, finely chopped
10 mint leaves, chopped

3. While you're waiting for the *kik alicha*, get started on the atakilt wat. Put the olive oil and onion in a skillet or frying pan and sauté over a high heat for a couple of minutes, stirring occasionally. Add the garlic and a little salt and pepper and cook over medium–high heat for a couple of minutes. Add the carrots, cumin and turmeric and cook for a few minutes, before adding the cabbage and cooking for about 5 minutes, stirring regularly. Mix in the potatoes and water, reduce the heat to medium–low, cover with a lid and simmer, stirring occasionally, for 15–20 minutes or until the potatoes are soft.

4. To make the cucumber and yogurt salad, put the cucumber, yogurt, onion and mint in a bowl with a little salt and pepper and mix well. Cover and leave in the fridge to chill.

5. To finish the *injera*, add 60ml/2fl oz/4 tbsp warm water, the salt, vinegar and baking powder and mix well. It should resemble a pancake batter. Drizzle the olive oil into a hot skillet or frying pan over a medium–high heat, moving it around so the oil covers the bottom of the pan (use a piece of paper towel to spread it). Pour in 2–3 tablespoons of the batter (you want quite a large, thin flatbread), tipping the pan so it is spread evenly, and wait until bubbles start to form. Leave for a minute or so and then flip it over and cook for a couple of minutes on the other side. Remove from the skillet, transfer to a plate and repeat until there's no more batter. If the mixture starts sticking, use the oily paper towel to reseason the bottom of the pan.

6. Serve one *injera* as the base to each plate or bowl and pile high with the *kik alicha*, *atakilt wat* and the cucumber yogurt salad. Keep any extra *injera* to eat on the side; it's traditionally used as the utensil instead of a knife and fork.

Vegan option Use a plant-based yogurt in the salad.

GOAT'S CHEESE, SAMPHIRE AND NEW POTATO FRITTATA

SERVES 2
WF / GF

30g/1oz/2 tbsp butter
1 onion, chopped
3 baby leeks, sliced
1 garlic clove, crushed
3 sprigs rosemary, chopped
400g/14oz new potatoes, boiled and
cut into chunks
salt and black pepper
85g/3oz samphire
6 eggs
100g/3½oz goat's cheese, crumbled

This frittata is one of our favourites for the skillet: a delicious and very easy to prepare meal. We adore the succulent saltiness of samphire and it's an ingredient that works beautifully with eggs. This frittata is perfect served with some mixed leaves and dressing.

1. Preheat the grill to 200°C/400°F.

2. Melt the butter in a skillet or frying pan, add the onion and sauté over a high heat for about 3 minutes. Add the leeks and cook for a further 3 minutes, stirring occasionally. Add the garlic and rosemary and cook for another 3 minutes. Add the potatoes, a little black pepper and a small pinch of salt (not too much as the samphire is quite salty) and cook for 4 minutes, stirring regularly to prevent catching, and then add the samphire and cook for another minute or two while you crack the eggs into a bowl and thoroughly whisk.

3. Pour the eggs into the pan, turn the heat down to low and sprinkle over the goat's cheese. Cook for a couple of minutes and then place under the grill for about 10 minutes until the cheese is golden. Poke it with a fork to make sure the eggs are cooked. Serve hot.

FEIJOADA WITH SPRING GREENS AND SMOKED TOFU

SERVES 4
V / WF / GF

Feijoada is a black bean stew that's a really big deal in Brazil. We've got fond memories of watching families in Trancoso queuing up for their Sunday hit of it; it's traditionally made with beef or pork, but we couldn't resist coming up with a meat-free take. Consider this smoked tofu version as a great vegan way of doing Sunday lunch, especially if the weather is kind enough to let you eat outdoors. We love the Taifun brand of smoked tofu but there are many others. This is lovely served with wholegrain rice or couscous.

2 small onions, chopped

2 carrots, diced

1 red pepper, deseeded and diced

1 tbsp olive oil

2 garlic cloves, crushed

1 tsp fresh or dried thyme

2 tsp sweet paprika

½ tsp ground cumin

1 sweet potato, diced

400g (1 can) chopped tomatoes

400g (1 can) black beans

2 bay leaves

400ml/14fl oz/1 ⅔ cups water

salt and black pepper

200g/7oz spring greens (collard greens), stems removed, finely sliced

100g/3½oz smoked tofu, diced

short-grain brown rice or wholegrain couscous, cooked, to serve

1. Place the onions, carrots, red pepper and olive oil in a Dutch oven or large pan over a medium heat and sauté for 3–5 minutes, stirring occasionally. Mix in the garlic, thyme, paprika, cumin and sweet potato and cook for a minute before adding the tomatoes, black beans (add the whole can, including the liquid), bay leaves and water. Cover with a lid and bring to the boil, then turn the heat down and simmer for about 40 minutes.

2. Remove the lid, season to taste with a little salt and pepper and cook for a further 10 minutes or so to thicken slightly, stirring occasionally.

3. Mix in the spring greens and smoked tofu and turn the heat up to bring it back to the boil, stirring regularly. Cook for a further 2–3 minutes, taste and adjust the seasoning and serve.

FREEKEH RISOTTO WITH ARTICHOKE HEARTS, RICOTTA, LEMON AND MINT

SERVES 2

Freekeh is one of our favourites among the ancient grains. It's a young green wheat that has been toasted and cracked and it's high in fibre, protein and many other essential nutrients. It still has a little bite to it even when fully cooked and we think it's a wonderful option for creating a wholegrain risotto.

200g/7oz/1 cup wholegrain freekeh
1½ tbsp butter
1 tbsp olive oil, plus extra to garnish
1 onion, chopped
salt and black pepper
1 large garlic clove, crushed
100ml/3½fl oz/scant ½ cup white wine
300ml/10fl oz/1¼ cups vegetable stock
185g/6½oz artichoke hearts, halved
185g/6½oz broad beans (fava beans)
60g/2oz/¼ cup ricotta, plus extra to garnish
10g/⅓oz mint, finely chopped, plus 2 sprigs to garnish
juice of ¼ lemon, plus 2 wedges to garnish

1. Soak the freekeh in cold water for about 5 minutes and then drain it in a sieve and run cold water over it for 5 minutes. Drain, briefly running cold water over it to rinse, and place to one side.

2. Meanwhile, heat the butter and olive oil in a wide, heavy-bottomed saucepan over a medium heat, add the onion and sauté for 3–4 minutes until translucent, stirring occasionally. Add a little salt and pepper and the garlic and sauté for another couple of minutes. Add the freekeh and the wine and cook for 3 minutes, then add the stock, cover with a lid, and bring to the boil. Reduce the heat to low and cook for 15 minutes, stirring occasionally. Add the artichokes and broad beans and cook for another 10 minutes, stirring occasionally.

3. Turn off the heat and add the ricotta and mint. Taste and adjust the seasoning, add the lemon juice, mix, and you're ready to serve. Finish with a drizzle of olive oil, a sprig of mint and wedge of lemon and a small extra dollop of ricotta.

GALLO PINTO BOWL WITH SWEET PLANTAIN, AVOCADO, GRILLED HALLOUMI AND A FRIED EGG

We were lucky enough to travel through Nicaragua and Costa Rica recently and one of our most abiding memories has to be of *gallo pinto*. The national dish of Costa Rica, served with every single meal, *gallo pinto* – or rice and beans – is truly ubiquitous, but it's so hearty and delicious you somehow never get tired of it. This bowl is inspired by our daily Nicaraguan breakfast. It's a true breakfast of champions but it works at any time of the day.

When shopping for plantains, remember that the blacker the skin, the sweeter the taste. You can substitute bananas if plantains are hard to come by.

SERVES 4
WF / GF

3 tbsp olive oil

1½ onions, chopped

2 garlic cloves, finely chopped

500g/1lb 2oz/2¾ cups long-grain brown rice

1.5 litres/2½ pints/1½ quarts vegetable stock

400g (1 can) black beans, drained

handful coriander (cilantro), chopped

salt and cracked black pepper

For the plantains

1 tbsp lightly salted butter

2 plantains, peeled and cut into diagonal slices

To serve

250g/9oz halloumi, cut into 8 slices

4 eggs

2 avocados, sliced

1 lime, cut into 4 wedges

1. Heat the olive oil in a large pan, add the onions and sauté for a couple of minutes until translucent. Add the garlic and the rice and sauté for another couple of minutes, stirring constantly.

2. Add the stock, cover the pan with a lid and bring to the boil. Boil for 25–30 minutes or until you can't see any stock. Mix in the beans, turn down the heat and simmer gently until the rice is fully cooked; this should take a further 10–15 minutes. Stir through the coriander, season with salt and pepper to taste and place to one side.

3. For the plantains, melt the butter in a skillet or frying pan and add the plantain slices. Cook over a medium heat until they're golden on the first side, then flip them over to brown the other side. Remove from the pan and place to one side.

4. In the same skillet or pan, melt a touch more butter if needed and cook the halloumi slices until they're golden on the first side, flip them over and cook the other side. Remove from the pan and place to one side.

5. Finally, in the same skillet or pan, melt a touch more butter if needed and fry the eggs.

6. To serve, scoop a generous amount of the rice and beans into each bowl and place the plantain, halloumi and avocado slices around the sides. Top with a fried egg and garnish with a wedge of lime.

MEXICAN BEAN POT BOWL WITH CITRUS CHARD

SERVES 4
VO / WF / GF

This is a really hearty bowl of food, loaded with a classic combination of black beans and kidney beans, peppers, corn and tomatoes, spiced up with smoky chipotle chilli. The citrus greens add a zesty lightness to the dish as well as a vitamin boost. We love rainbow chard, both for its taste and its cheery looks, but normal chard is fine, as is kale, cavolo nero or any other favourite greens.

1 tbsp olive oil
2 small onions, chopped
3 garlic cloves, crushed
1 green pepper, diced
1 tbsp dried oregano
salt and black pepper
1 tsp sweet paprika
½ dried chipotle chilli, soaked in hot water until soft, drained and chopped
1 tsp ground cumin
400g (1 can) chopped tomatoes
400g (1 can) black beans, drained
400g (1 can) red kidney beans, drained
400ml/14fl oz/1 ⅔ cups water
75g/2½oz soya chunks, soaked in hot water until soft, drained
1 corn on the cob, kernels removed
handful coriander (cilantro), chopped, plus extra to garnish

For the citrus chard
1 tbsp olive oil
200g/7oz chard, roughly chopped
½ lime

To serve
short-grain brown rice or quinoa, cooked
4 lime wedges
150ml/5fl oz/⅔ cup sour cream

1. Put the olive oil and onions in a large pan or Dutch oven and sauté over a high heat for a couple of minutes. Add the garlic, green pepper, oregano and a little salt and pepper and sauté for a few more minutes, stirring regularly until the vegetables have taken on a little colour. Stir in the paprika, chipotle, cumin, tomatoes, black beans, kidney beans and water. Cover with a lid and bring to the boil, then turn the heat down to low and simmer for about 1 hour, stirring occasionally.

2. Add the soya chunks and simmer for about 25 minutes. Add the corn and coriander and simmer for 5 minutes. Taste and adjust the seasoning.

3. When the bean pot is nearly ready, prepare the citrus chard: heat the olive oil in a wok over a high heat, add the chard and cook for a couple of minutes, moving the greens around regularly and adding a generous pinch of salt and pepper. Squeeze over the lime juice.

4. Serve the bean pot over rice or quinoa, with the citrus chard on the side. Garnish with a lime wedge, a dollop of sour cream and some coriander.

Vegan option Omit the sour cream or use a substitute.

POKE NERO BOWL WITH TAMARI-BAKED TOFU, SEA VEGETABLE SALAD AND BLACK RICE

SERVES 2
V / WF / GF

We love anything that revolves around putting lots of good stuff in a bowl and 'poke' is a concept for this that seems to be rather in vogue at the moment. Originating from Hawaii, poke normally involves raw fish, but we've gone with a tofu version. Black rice (the 'nero' in this poke nero) is as sexy as rice can get. Its showstopping looks are highlighted by the greens and purples of the sea vegetables. We love the Clearspring brand's sea vegetable salad but there are other brands around and you could also try using wakame or dulse. Seaweeds are a brilliant way to get iodine into your diet, along with concentrated amounts of other minerals and nutrients.

15g/½oz fresh root ginger, finely grated

6 tbsp tamari

2 tbsp agave

½ small red chilli, finely chopped

400g/14oz fresh firm tofu, cut into bite-sized cubes

1½ tbsp brown rice vinegar

2 tsp mirin

1 tsp sesame oil

½ cucumber, very thinly sliced (ideally on a mandolin)

10g/⅓oz dried sea vegetable salad, soaked in cold water for about 10 minutes, then drained

salt and black pepper

250g/9oz/1 ⅓ cups black rice, cooked

2 tsp black sesame seeds

1 spring onion (scallion), green part only, finely sliced

1. Preheat the oven to 200°C/400°F/Gas 6. Line a roasting tray with greaseproof (waxed) paper.

2. Put the ginger, 4 tablespoons of the tamari, the agave and chilli in a bowl and mix. Add the tofu and mix so the cubes are well coated and then transfer them to the lined roasting tray and bake for about 30 minutes. Move the tofu around every 10 minutes or so to prevent sticking.

3. While that's baking, make the sea vegetable salad. Combine the remaining 2 tablespoons of tamari with the vinegar, mirin and sesame oil. Add the cucumber and sea vegetables and a little salt and pepper and leave to one side.

4. To serve, place the rice in the bowls, spoon over some of the baked tofu and top with the sea vegetable salad and a sprinkle of black sesame seeds and spring onion.

RENDANG-STYLE CURRY BOWL WITH AUBERGINE, GREEN BEANS AND SOYA CHUNKS

This delicious curry is inspired by the curry paste traditionally used to make rendang, a spicy meat curry that originated in Western Sumatra. Our vegan version doesn't quite have the rich red colour of the classic beef one (although the paprika helps) and we've moderated the spice (if you like it hot, add one or two more bird's eye chillies to the paste) but there's no compromise on taste and it seemed a shame for us veggies to miss out on a truly mighty curry. We love using aubergines, green beans and soya chunks (available in all health food stores) but another interesting and traditional option to consider is jackfruit, if you can get your hands on one.

SERVES 4
V / WF / GF

For the spice paste
1 tsp cumin seeds
½ tsp coriander seeds
3 green cardamom pods, seeds only
¼ tsp turmeric
1 tsp sweet paprika
3 dried red chillies, deseeded
1 onion, roughly chopped
10g/⅓oz fresh root ginger, roughly chopped
3 garlic cloves, roughly chopped
10g/⅓oz coriander root, roughly chopped
15g/½oz lemongrass, finely chopped
4 dried kaffir lime leaves
10g/⅓oz galangal, roughly chopped
1 bird's eye chilli, roughly chopped
100ml/3½fl oz/scant ½ cup water

1. Begin by making the spice paste. In a hot dry pan, lightly toast the cumin, coriander and cardamom seeds until they're fragrant. Transfer to a pestle and mortar and crush to a powder. Add the turmeric and paprika and mix.

2. In a blender, place the dried chillies, onion, ginger, garlic, coriander root, lemongrass, kaffir lime leaves, galangal and bird's eye chilli, along with the spices from the pestle and mortar and the water, and blend to a fine paste.

3. To make the curry, heat 2 tablespoons of the coconut oil in a saucepan and add the spice paste. Cook the paste over a medium heat, stirring regularly for about 5 minutes or until it starts to take on some colour. Add the sugar and cook for a couple of minutes, still stirring regularly. Turn the heat down to low, add the coconut milk and tamari, cover with a lid and heat for about 10 minutes, stirring occasionally. Add the aubergine, cover, and cook for another 10 minutes, stirring regularly.

For the curry

3 tbsp coconut oil

20g/¾oz/1½ tbsp light muscovado or other unrefined brown sugar

800ml (2 cans) coconut milk

2 tbsp tamari

1 aubergine (eggplant), diced

150g/5½oz green beans, topped and tailed, steamed

4 small shallots, halved

salt

100g/3½oz soya chunks, soaked in hot water until soft, drained

handful coriander (cilantro), roughly chopped

To serve

short-grain brown rice, cooked

1 batch cucumber pickle (optional, page 109)

handful crisp-fried onions or shallots (optional)

4. Meanwhile, heat the remaining coconut oil in a frying pan over a high heat, add the green beans, shallots and a pinch of salt and stir them around occasionally until they start to take on some colour. Add them to the curry pan along with the soya chunks and fresh coriander and cook over a medium heat, without a lid, for 30–40 minutes, stirring occasionally.

5. When the curry is ready, serve on a bed of brown rice. If using, place a little cucumber pickle to one side and garnish with crispy shallots.

SRI LANKAN CURRY BOWL

SERVES 4
V / WF / GF

We fell completely in love with Sri Lanka on a recent visit and were determined to recreate some of the fabulous food we had enjoyed as soon as we got home. This curry is based on one we were shown by one of our hosts; it's just a shame we can't go and pick fresh curry leaves straight from the jungle as he did, nor pop to the garden for a coconut. It's a great dish on its own, but the sambols traditionally served alongside were also to die for and if you've got time to make up our simple recipe for *pol sambol* (page 116), it really elevates this dish.

1 tsp coriander seeds

1 tsp cumin seeds

½ tsp fennel seeds

½ tsp turmeric

½ tsp chilli powder

2 tsp mustard seeds

1 tbsp coconut oil

1 large onion, roughly chopped

2 garlic cloves, finely chopped

1½ tsp rapadura sugar or other unrefined brown sugar

400ml (1 can) coconut milk

20 curry leaves

1 sweet potato, cut into chunks

250ml/9fl oz/1 cup water

1 small cauliflower, cut into bite-sized florets

125g/4½oz okra, trimmed

1½ tbsp tamari

handful coriander (cilantro), roughly chopped

juice of 1 lime

To serve

wholegrain basmati rice, cooked

100g/3½oz/¾ cup cashews, roasted

1 batch *pol sambol* (optional, page 116)

1. In a hot dry pan, lightly toast the coriander, cumin and fennel seeds until they're fragrant. Transfer to a pestle and mortar, add the turmeric and chilli powder, and grind to a powder.

2. In the dry pan, over a medium heat, lightly toast the mustard seeds until they release their aroma. Add the coconut oil and once it's melted add the onion and sauté for a couple of minutes or so until translucent. Add the garlic, sugar and the powdered spices. Turn the heat down to low and cook for a couple of minutes, stirring constantly. Add the coconut milk and curry leaves and cook, stirring occasionally, for about 3 minutes. Add the sweet potato and the water, cover with a lid and turn the heat up to high until it comes to the boil, and then down to low, and simmer, stirring occasionally, for about 20 minutes. Add the cauliflower, okra and tamari and cook for a further 10 minutes or until the vegetables are tender.

3. Add the chopped coriander and lime juice and serve over basmati rice with a few cashews and a little *pol sambol*, if using.

SWEET POTATO, CHARD AND BURNT TOMATO HASH

SERVES 2
WF / GF

30g/1oz/2 tbsp butter

1 onion, sliced

salt and black pepper

1 leek, white part only, thinly sliced

1 garlic clove, finely chopped

2 tsp dried rosemary or 1 tsp fresh rosemary, chopped

150g/5½oz swiss chard, roughly chopped

600g/1lb 5oz sweet potato, grated (we leave the skins on)

50g/1¾oz feta cheese, crumbled

2 eggs

10 cherry tomatoes

This skillet hash is one of our favourite camping recipes and is one we turn to again and again to keep us going while we're setting up for festivals. While you just can't beat the taste of food cooked over an open fire, this can of course also be made at home and it is an ideal dish for cosy nights in. It's supreme comfort food but also super easy and uses only one pan.

1. Heat the butter in a skillet or a heavy-bottomed frying pan, add the onion and ½ teaspoon of salt, turn down the heat (if you're cooking at home rather than on an open flame) and leave to caramelize for about 10 minutes, stirring occasionally.

2. Add the leek, garlic, rosemary and a little pepper and leave to caramelize for a further 10 minutes, stirring occasionally.

3. Add the chard and, still stirring every now and then, cook for a couple of minutes to wilt the chard. Add the sweet potato and cook for a further 10–15 minutes, still stirring regularly to prevent catching.

4. Mix in the feta and then make two hollows in the mixture and crack an egg into each hollow. Cover with a lid and cook for about 10 minutes until the eggs are done.

5. Meanwhile, place the cherry tomatoes either on some embers if you're outdoors or, if you're cooking at home, one at a time, directly on the open flame of the hob, until they're well charred. Remove carefully with tongs, add to the skillet once the eggs are cooked, and you're ready to serve.

YELLOW TAGINE BOWL WITH KAMUT COUSCOUS

SERVES 4–6
VO

We're very keen on salty and sweet combinations and so love the apricots, preserved lemons and raisins in this dish. Rose harissa is an ingredient we're seriously mad about: a deeply aromatic Middle Eastern spice paste, the gentle heat of the chilli coupled with the sweet smokiness of the red peppers and rose petals adds real depth to this tagine. We serve this with kamut couscous, which can be found in health food stores (we use the Lima brand), but there's no problem using wholewheat couscous as an alternative.

1 large sweet potato, peeled and diced
1 small butternut squash, peeled and diced
5 small carrots, sliced
4 tbsp olive oil, plus extra to serve
2 small onions, sliced
3 garlic cloves, crushed
½ tsp cumin seeds
¼ tsp coriander seeds
400g (1 can) chopped tomatoes
2 bay leaves
1 tbsp honey
1 tbsp rose harissa
15 apricots (ideally unsulphured), halved
30g/1oz/3 tbsp raisins
400g (1 can) chickpeas, drained
skin of 1 preserved lemon, thinly sliced
400ml/14fl oz/1 ⅔ cups water
salt and black pepper

To serve

500g/1lb 2oz/scant 3 cups kamut couscous or other wholegrain couscous
600ml/20fl oz/2½ cups water
250g/9oz/1 cup natural yogurt
45g/1½oz/6 tbsp flaked (sliced) almonds, toasted
8 sprigs coriander (cilantro)

1. Preheat the oven to 200°C/400°F/Gas 6.

2. In a large bowl, mix the sweet potato, butternut squash and carrots with 3 tablespoons of olive oil. Tip the vegetables into a hot pan and sauté for 7–8 minutes until they've taken on some lovely charred colour (do this in batches if you don't have a large enough pan). Remove from the heat and place to one side.

3. Put a casserole dish or Dutch oven over a high heat, add the remaining olive oil and the onions and sauté for a couple of minutes. Add the garlic, cumin and coriander – and a dash more olive oil if necessary – and continue to cook for a couple of minutes, stirring regularly. Turn the heat down to medium and then add the tomatoes, bay leaves, honey, harissa, apricots, raisins, chickpeas, preserved lemon, water, a generous pinch of salt and pepper and the charred vegetables. Mix, then turn the heat back to high and cook for 3–4 minutes. Cover the casserole with a lid and place in the oven for 60 minutes.

4. Meanwhile, cook the couscous. Bring the water to the boil in a pan, add the couscous and turn off the heat. Cover with a lid and leave for at least 10–15 minutes until it's soft and fluffy (it's OK if you leave it longer).

5. Serve the tagine over the couscous, drizzle over a little olive oil, swirl in a dollop of yogurt and top with flaked almonds, coriander sprigs and additional seasoning to taste.

Vegan option Use brown sugar in place of honey and either omit the yogurt or use a plant-based yogurt.

For the tandoori paneer

½ tsp coriander seeds

1 tsp smoked paprika

1 tsp turmeric

1 tsp ground cumin

½ tsp chilli powder

½ tsp ground black pepper

½ tsp salt

1 green cardamom pod, seeds only

2 garlic cloves, crushed

10g/⅓oz fresh root ginger, grated

1 tbsp olive oil

juice of 1½ lemons

226g (1 pack) paneer, cut into about 15 cubes

For the pineapple *pachadi*

½ pineapple, peeled and cut into small chunks

100ml/3½fl oz/scant ½ cup water

¼ tsp ground cumin

½ tsp turmeric

½ tsp chilli powder

45g/1½oz/½ cup desiccated coconut

salt and black pepper

½ tbsp coconut oil

½ tsp mustard seeds

10 curry leaves

200g/7oz/generous ¾ cup natural yogurt

To serve

250g/9oz/1⅓ cups red rice, cooked

4 sprigs coriander (cilantro)

2 lemon wedges

TANDOORI PANEER BOWL WITH PINEAPPLE PACHADI AND RED RICE

We serve halloumi with our signature Buddha bowls and it really does seem to be the cheese that nobody can get enough of, but we reckon paneer has a similar kind of a vibe going on. Paneer is a fresh, unsalted cheese that is a star ingredient in many south Asian cuisines; understandable, as its soft milky flavour works so well with the otherwise strong flavours of those cuisines. It's also super-versatile: it doesn't melt, so it can be skewered, crumbled or cut into cubes and added to soups or curries. It's easy enough to track down these days, or you can make your own, using whole milk and a muslin cloth.

In this dish the spiced paneer is served alongside nutty-tasting red rice and creamy *pachadi* – a yogurt-based south Indian condiment. The red rice looks incredible but you can use any rice of your choice.

1. Begin by making the spice mix for the paneer. Toast the coriander seeds in a hot dry pan until they are aromatic and then put them in a mixing bowl along with the paprika, turmeric, cumin, chilli powder, pepper, salt and cardamom. Mix and then transfer to a coffee grinder or pestle and mortar and grind to a powder. Tip the powder back into the mixing bowl, add the garlic, ginger, olive oil and lemon juice and mix thoroughly. Add the paneer cubes and thoroughly coat with the spice mix, cover with clingfilm (plastic wrap) and leave to marinate for at least 30 minutes – ideally longer (even overnight in the fridge if you're very organized).

2. Preheat the grill to 200°C/400°F.

3. Meanwhile, make the *pachadi*. Place the pineapple in a pan with the water, cumin, turmeric and chilli powder, cover with a lid and bring to the boil. Once boiling, turn the heat down to medium and cook for 15 minutes or so, stirring occasionally. If it gets too dry, add a little more water. Transfer three quarters of the mix to a blender, pulse until smooth and then pour back over the remaining pineapple. Add the coconut and a touch of salt and pepper and leave to cool for 5 minutes.

Method continues overleaf >>

4. While it's cooling, melt the coconut oil in a pan over a medium–high heat, add the mustard seeds and curry leaves and leave to splutter for a couple of minutes. Place to one side. Stir the yogurt into the pineapple mix and pour the mustard seeds and curry leaves over the top. Season with a little more salt and pepper and leave to one side.

5. Transfer the paneer cubes and all the marinade into a skillet or roasting tray and place under the grill for 15–20 minutes, turning every now and again. You want it to take on a slightly charred appearance, but not too much.

6. Serve the red rice in bowls, add the paneer and the *pachadi* and garnish with coriander and a wedge of lemon.

Vegan option Go for fresh tofu instead of paneer and use a plant-based yogurt in the *pachadi*.

YUCATÁN SALBUTES WITH SOYA MINCE, CABBAGE SLAW, AVOCADO AND FETA SMASH AND PICKLED RED ONIONS

SERVES 2
AS A MAIN
OR 4 AS A
SMALL BITE
V WITHOUT
THE FETA

Everybody has their happy place, the one your mind immediately turns to when you're asked to visualize yourself in paradise. The beach in Tulum is one of ours and images of sunny days and rolling waves turn quickly to memories of the excellent vegan food at a fine establishment in the jungle called Restaurare. This is where we first tried *salbutes*, heavenly little puffed tortillas. At home, we realized they weren't so hard to make. You'll need to track down masa harina flour (a type of flour made from corn kernels and a staple in any Mexican kitchen), in health food shops; it's also available online. It can be quite variable from brand to brand – we use the Cool Chile Co's for best results.

The *salbutes* are always served with avocado and this smash (which we also love on toast for an easy, healthy breakfast) goes perfectly. They're also not the real deal unless topped with pink pickled onions; these can be made in advance and are excellent to have around to jazz up all kinds of dishes.

For the pink pickled onions

2 red onions, finely sliced

1 tbsp sea salt

½ tsp coriander seeds

pinch of cumin seeds

½ tsp black peppercorns

1 bay leaf

250ml/9fl oz/1 cup apple cider vinegar

For the soya mince filling

2 tbsp olive oil

1 onion, chopped

pinch of salt

cracked black pepper

1 garlic clove, finely chopped

½ green pepper, chopped

¼ dried chipotle chilli, soaked in hot water until soft, drained and chopped

½ tsp ground cumin

pinch of ground cinnamon

85g/3oz dried soya mince, soaked in hot water until soft, drained

200g/7oz/scant 1 cup canned chopped tomatoes

100ml/3½fl oz/scant ½ cup red wine or water

Ingredients continue overleaf >>

1. Begin by making the pickled onions. Put the onions and salt in a large bowl, mix thoroughly and leave to one side for about 20 minutes.

2. Transfer the onions to a jar along with the coriander seeds, cumin seeds, peppercorns and bay leaf. Pour over the vinegar, seal the jar, and then leave for at least 45 minutes until they're a nice translucent pink colour. After 45 minutes, they'll be yummy and ready to eat but they just get better the longer you leave them. You can make them well in advance and store them in the fridge.

3. To make the soya mince filling, heat the olive oil in a saucepan, add the onion and sauté until it starts to look translucent. Add the salt, a little black pepper and then add the garlic, green pepper and chipotle and sauté for 5 minutes, stirring occasionally. Add the cumin and cinnamon and sauté for a couple of minutes. Add the mince and brown for 5 minutes, stirring regularly to prevent catching.

Method continues overleaf >>

For the shredded cabbage slaw

½ white cabbage (about 400g/14oz), finely shredded

juice of 1 lime

good pinch of salt

handful coriander (cilantro), chopped

For the avocado and feta smash

1 ripe avocado, roughly chopped

100g/3½oz feta, roughly chopped

juice of ¼ lime

For the *salbutes*

100g/3½oz/scant 1 cup masa harina flour

½ tsp baking powder

pinch of salt

1 tbsp wholemeal self-raising flour

¼ tsp sweet paprika

250ml/9fl oz/1 cup vegetable oil, for frying

To serve

50g/1¾oz/4–5 tbsp mixed seeds (such as pumpkin, sesame, sunflower, flax, poppy), lightly toasted

1 lime, cut into wedges

a few sprigs coriander (cilantro)

Add the tomatoes and wine or water and cook until the mixture is quite dry, stirring regularly, for about 10 minutes. Taste and season, then place to one side.

4. To make the slaw, just mix everything together in a bowl, then place to one side.

5. To make the avocado smash, put everything in a bowl and smash it all together with a fork, adding salt and pepper to taste. Great for stress relief. Put to the side.

6. Now you're ready to make the *salbutes*. It's important to make these last so that they can be served straight away while they're still hot and nicely puffed up.

7. Put all the ingredients (except the vegetable oil) in a large bowl and then knead in just enough water to create a pliable dough; around 200ml/7fl oz/¾ cup water. Roll the dough into 30–40g/1–1½oz balls (about the size of a table tennis ball). Take a ball and (unless you're already kitted out with a tortilla press) place it inside a sandwich bag, then flatten it with your hands until it's very thin, about 2mm. Remove from the bag and repeat the process until you've flattened all the balls.

8. In a frying pan or skillet, heat the vegetable oil to about 190°C/375°F and then carefully put one of the *salbutes* into the oil. You'll know if the oil is hot enough because the *salbute* will quickly rise to the top and start ballooning straight away. After about 15 seconds, flip it over with a pair of tongs to cook the other side. When it's beautifully golden on both sides, remove it from the oil and drain on paper towels. Repeat until all the *salbutes* are cooked.

9. To serve, place 3–5 *salbutes* on each plate. Top with a generous spoonful of the soya mince filling, and then one of the slaw and finally a spoonful of the smash. Place a few slices of pickled onions on top of each *salbute* and garnish with the toasted seeds, lime wedges and coriander sprigs. They can be a bit messy to eat but are absolutely delicious!

SWEET POTATO AND COCONUT POLENTA BOWL WITH ASIAN GREENS AND WILD MUSHROOMS

Polenta is a great ingredient to get to grips with and is brilliant if you're looking for ways to avoid wheat and gluten. Common in Italian cuisine (and also widely used in America to make cornbreads), it's basically just boiled cornmeal and can be enjoyed either as a kind of porridge or mashed potato sort of thing, as we do in this recipe, or left to cool and solidify into a loaf that can be baked, grilled or fried. It's sometimes accused of being a little bland, but the addition of coconut milk remedies that and gives an Asian twist that's compounded by the wild mushrooms, tamari and Asian greens. Greens-wise, we tend to use pak choi but gai lan is another favourite.

SERVES 2
V / WF / GF

2 small sweet potatoes, diced
500ml/18fl oz/2 cups vegetable stock
150g/5½oz green beans, topped and tailed
400ml (1 can) coconut milk
salt and black pepper
150g/5½/1¼ cups polenta
1 tbsp coconut oil
1 small onion, sliced
2 garlic cloves, crushed
15g/½oz fresh root ginger, chopped
½ long red chilli, chopped
1 tsp unrefined brown sugar
30g/1oz dried wild mushrooms, soaked in 500ml/18fl oz/2 cups boiling water for 15 minutes, then strained, keeping the water
2 pak choi, sliced into large pieces
1½ tbsp tamari
30g/1oz/3 tbsp pumpkin seeds, toasted

1. Put the sweet potatoes and stock in a pan, cover with a lid and cook over a high heat until the potatoes are soft; this should take about 15 minutes.

2. Meanwhile, bring a small pan of water to the boil, add the green beans and blanch for about 3 minutes. Drain and run them under cold water to stop the cooking process, drain again and place to one side.

3. Once the sweet potatoes are cooked, transfer the contents of the pan to a blender and blend until smooth. Put this mixture back into the pan, add the coconut milk and a pinch of salt and bring to the boil, stirring occasionally. Stir in the polenta, turn the heat down and cook for 5 minutes, stirring constantly. Cover with a lid and place to one side.

4. Put the coconut oil into a hot wok over a high heat, add the onion and sauté for 1 minute, then add the garlic, ginger and chilli and stir-fry for a further minute before adding the sugar, mushrooms, green beans and pak choi. Stir-fry for about 3 minutes, then add the tamari and 100ml/3½fl oz/scant ½ cup of the water you soaked the mushrooms in and stir-fry for a couple of minutes before removing from the heat.

5. Place the polenta in serving bowls and top with the vegetables. Sprinkle over the pumpkin seeds and season to taste with a little salt and black pepper.

BUDDHA BOWLS
Enlightened Eating

Every Bowl contains:-
- Massaman curry with new potatos, pineapple and soya chunks
- Carrot and homemade kimchi pickle
- Flash steamed seasonal greens
- Organic shortgrain brown rice
- Omega seed sprinkle

BABY BUDDHA - £6 ♥ BIG BUDDHA - £7

Add Halloumi - £1

veggie ♥ vegan ♥ wheat free ♥ gluten free

CHAPTER 5
ACCOMPANIMENTS
AND SIDES

BASIC KIMCHI

This needs a bit of time to ferment but otherwise it's easy to make. Most commercial brands of kimchi include fish sauce among the ingredients, so it's good to know how to prepare it yourself. Kimchi has numerous well-documented health benefits as a result of being fermented and it's packed full of good bacteria, so it's especially good for digestive health and immunity. We eat a bit of something fermented with many of our meals, not least our signature Buddha bowls (page 66).

Once you've got the hang of a basic kimchi, you can begin to experiment with using other vegetables. Root vegetables like daikon (mooli), beetroot, turnip and radish are all very suitable for making kimchi.

MAKES ABOUT 750G/1LB 10OZ
V / WF / GF

30g/1oz/scant 2 tbsp sea salt

1 litre/1¾ pints/4 cups water

1 Chinese leaf (napa cabbage), stalk removed, sliced

3 spring onions (scallions), sliced

1 carrot, shaved into strips using a potato peeler

5 long red chillies, stalks removed

60g/2oz fresh root ginger, roughly chopped

9 garlic cloves

1. Place the salt and water in a 2.5 litre/4½ pint/2½ quart preserving jar and stir well to dissolve the salt. Add the Chinese leaf, spring onions and carrot, pushing them down so they all fit snugly in; discard any that you can't squeeze in. Seal the jar and leave for about 12 hours or overnight.

2. Once that's ready, make the chilli paste by putting the chillies, ginger, garlic and 200ml/7fl oz/¾ cup water in a food processor or blender and blending until they're well combined. Place to one side.

3. Drain off about two thirds of the brine from the jar, reserving the drained-off brine. Pour the chilli paste into the jar and, using a long metal spoon, make sure it's all well mixed and pushed down so there's a little bit of space at the top of the jar. Place about 200ml/7fl oz/¾ cup (doesn't have to be precise) of the reserved brine into a sandwich bag, seal it, and place it on top of the vegetables in the jar before resealing the jar. This keeps the vegetables submerged, which prevents the top layer from going off.

4. Leave the jar out but keep it away from direct sunlight. Taste every few days and when it's a little bit fizzy and tastes really good, usually after 1–2 weeks, it's ready. Remove the sandwich bag and store the kimchi in the fridge. It should keep for at least a couple of weeks.

CARROT AND KIMCHI PICKLE

SERVES 4
AS A SIDE
V / WF / GF

This is how we use kimchi in our signature Buddha bowls. It's also a fabulous accompaniment to many other things: as a side dish with curries, in wraps or sandwiches, with baked sweet potatoes or even with tacos.

The pickle juice part of the recipe makes a decent-sized batch, which can be kept for months in a sterilized jar in the fridge.

4 carrots, grated
125g/4½oz kimchi (see page 106)

For the pickle juice
125ml/4fl oz/½ cup apple cider vinegar
85g/3oz/scant ½ cup soft brown sugar
pinch of salt

1. First, make the pickle juice, put the vinegar, sugar and salt in a pan and bring to the boil, stirring occasionally to ensure the sugar doesn't burn. Remove from the heat and leave to cool. Once cool, place in a jar and store in the fridge.

2. Combine the grated carrots with the kimchi and spoon over approximately 4 tablespoons of the pickle juice. Leave it to pickle for about an hour before serving.

CUCUMBER PICKLE

SERVES 4
AS A SIDE
V / WF / GF

This is a pretty much instant pickle that adds a wonderful sweet tanginess to whatever you serve it with. We especially enjoy it alongside curries and tofu dishes. If you have a mandolin, you can get the cucumber wafer thin; alternatively, use a potato peeler to turn it into ribbons.

1 cucumber, thinly sliced
salt
2 tbsp brown rice vinegar
2 tsp mirin
3 tbsp sesame seeds, lightly toasted

Place the cucumber in a bowl. Add a generous pinch of salt and mix before adding the vinegar and mirin and finally the sesame seeds. Mix again and it's ready to eat.

BURNT ASPARAGUS WITH LEMONY MUSTARD BUTTER

SERVES 2
VO / WF / GF

250g/9oz asparagus (woody ends removed), steamed until just tender
45g/1½oz/3 tbsp butter
30g/1oz/2 tbsp wholegrain mustard
2 tbsp lemon juice
1 tsp honey
salt and black pepper

Yum! Asparagus is great no matter what, but this is a really simple way to turn it into a standout side dish or snack. At barbecues this normally makes the meat eaters more than a bit jealous.

Heat a skillet, frying pan or griddle pan; when it's very hot, add the steamed asparagus and allow to burn (slightly!) for a minute or so, gently moving it around every now and again until it just starts to blacken. Add the butter, mustard, lemon juice, honey and a pinch of salt and pepper. Once it's all melted, tip it into a serving dish.

Vegan option Use olive oil in place of butter and omit the honey.

FLASH-STEAMED SEASONAL GREENS

SERVES 2
AS A SIDE
V / WF / GF

A key component of our Buddha bowls, this is a super-easy way of cooking your greens and it eliminates any risk of them going soggy. Kale is the vegetable we use most, but spring greens (collard greens), chard or savoy cabbage are also great options.

200g/7oz greens
salt and black pepper

Place the greens in a hot dry wok or pan and add a ladleful of hot water, which will instantly steam them. After about 10–20 seconds they will be ready to serve, with a little salt and cracked black pepper.

HAZELNUT DUKKAH

MAKES
ABOUT
210G /7½OZ
V / WF / GF

Dukkah is a handy thing to have around the wholefood kitchen. You can use it as a healthy, protein-boosting sprinkle on all kinds of things, such as salads, soups or leafy greens. The traditional way is to serve it with a bowl of olive oil and your favourite bread. Dip a hunk of bread into the oil and then into the dukkah and you'll be in heaven. This is quite a simple recipe but you can let your imagination go wild and add all manner of nuts and spices. It will keep in a sealed jar for up to a month.

1 tsp fennel seeds
60g/2oz/scant ½ cup sesame seeds
1 tsp coriander seeds
150g/5½oz/generous 1 cup hazelnuts, roasted
salt and black pepper

In a hot dry pan, lightly toast the fennel seeds until they release their aroma. Place in a blender and then repeat with the sesame seeds. Place those in the blender too, and repeat with the coriander seeds. Put the coriander seeds in the blender along with the hazelnuts and a generous pinch of salt and pepper and blend until the mixture resembles breadcrumbs.

PINK KRAUT WITH JUNIPER BERRIES

MAKES
ABOUT
400G/14 OZ
V / WF / GF

This ferment is really easy to make and goes well with so many dishes. We pop some on our sandwiches and salads and it's delicious with a baked potato. But it's the pink colour that really cheers the soul and adds a welcome touch of vibrancy to any plate. It's a great alternative to kimchi if you're not too keen on chilli.

400g/14oz red cabbage, finely sliced or grated, reserving 2 leaves
15g/½oz/scant 1 tbsp salt, plus 1 tsp
25 dried juniper berries

1. Place the cabbage in a large mixing bowl along with 15g of the salt and the juniper berries. Mix well before transferring to a 1 litre/1¾ pint/4 cup preserving jar. Pack it in tightly, pushing the cabbage down in the jar for a few minutes to start to release the latent water from the cabbage. Place the 2 reserved leaves on top.

2. Mix 1 teaspoon of salt with about 225ml/8fl oz/scant 1 cup water and pour into the sandwich bag. Seal the sandwich bag and put it into the preserving jar to push the cabbage down before sealing the jar.

3. Store the jar away from direct sunlight. Taste every couple of days and when it's slightly fizzy and very yummy, it's ready; this usually takes 4–10 days. Once fermented, store in the fridge.

POL SAMBOL

SERVES 2–4
AS A SIDE
V / WF / GF

½ small red onion, finely chopped
60g/2oz/⅔ cup desiccated coconut
½ tsp red chilli flakes
juice of ½ lime
pinch of salt
pinch of pepper

This coconut sambol is served as a side to pretty much everything in Sri Lanka. The Sri Lankans' relationship to it is not unlike ours to ketchup, but its flavours, while simple, are certainly a little more palate-tingling: spicy, sour, sweet and salty, all at once. It's very straightforward to make and is best eaten fresh. It's great with our Sri Lankan curry (page 88).

Put all the ingredients together in a bowl and mix thoroughly with your hands.

SEENI SAMBOL

SERVES 2–4
AS A SIDE
V / WF / GF

1 tbsp coconut oil
2 red onions, finely sliced
½ tbsp light muscovado sugar or other unrefined brown sugar
1 tsp tamarind concentrate
3 green cardamom pods
1 cinnamon stick
1 tsp red chilli flakes (or 1 tbsp if you like it spicy)
1 handful curry leaves
2 cloves
pinch of salt

Sambols are handy condiments for perking up other dishes and making them truly knockout. This caramelized onion sambol is traditionally served in Sri Lanka alongside hoppers and breads but we also love it with curries and other rice dishes, and it's great with a boiled egg for a really easy breakfast. It's very straightforward to make and lasts for a couple of days in the fridge.

1. Melt the coconut oil in a pan, add the red onions and sweat over quite a high heat for about 5 minutes, stirring regularly. Add the sugar, tamarind, cardamom pods, cinnamon, chilli flakes, curry leaves, cloves and salt and sweat for a couple more minutes, stirring often.

2. Turn the heat down to low, cover with a lid and cook, stirring occasionally, for about 35 minutes. If the mixture starts to catch, just add a splash of water.

3. Leave to cool before serving or transferring to a jar to store.

ROASTED BUTTERNUT SQUASH WITH BROWN SUGAR AND CINNAMON

SERVES 2
AS A SIDE
V / WF / GF

This is a South African staple and is delicious served as an accompaniment to a main meal or at a barbecue, lending a touch of warming sweetness to whatever it's served alongside.

Gem squash are also good prepared in this way. Simply cut them in half widthways, scoop out the seeds and fill with some of the spice mix before roasting. Serve the squash with a dollop of crème fraîche if you like.

500g/1lb 2oz butternut squash, peeled and cut into bite-sized chunks
20g/¾oz/1½ tbsp unrefined brown sugar
4 tsp olive oil
1 tsp ground cinnamon
salt and black pepper

1. Preheat the oven to 200°C/400°F/Gas 6. Line a roasting tray with greaseproof (waxed) paper.

2. Mix all the ingredients together in a large bowl and then transfer to the lined roasting tray. Place in the oven and roast for 55–60 minutes or until cooked, turning the chunks of squash occasionally.

BARBECUE SAUCE

MAKES
ABOUT 400ML/
14FL OZ/2 CUPS
V / WF / GF

When eating outdoors it's a must to have a bottle of this to hand. It's also a great marinade for vegetables or tofu. It's surprisingly easy to make, and while there certainly are some good sauces available to buy, nothing beats homemade.

1 tbsp olive oil

3 garlic cloves, crushed

1 small onion, chopped

2 tbsp chopped fresh thyme

1 tbsp molasses

1 dried chipotle chilli, soaked in hot water until soft, drained and chopped

2 tbsp rum

2 tsp red wine vinegar

2 tbsp tamari

300ml/10fl oz/1¼ cups tomato ketchup

salt and black pepper

1. Heat the oil in a saucepan and sauté the garlic, onion and thyme for 2 minutes. Add the molasses and chipotle and leave to caramelize for a minute, then add the rum, vinegar and tamari and cook for 2 more minutes. Add the ketchup and a touch of salt and pepper and mix thoroughly, bring to the boil and then turn down the heat and simmer for 10–15 minutes, stirring occasionally.

2. Leave to cool before serving, or transfer to a bottle or jar if you want to store it for a few days.

LABNEH

MAKES
500G/
1LB 2OZ
WF / GF

This Middle Eastern cheese is a fantastic and versatile ingredient but it can be a little hard to track down. But don't let that put you off! It's actually super easy to make at yourself at home. It just needs to be left for 24 hours, so does need a little forward planning, but it's well worth it and is delicious served with salads, as part of a mezze platter or enjoyed on it's own with a basket of warm pitas.

muslin cloth
pinch of salt
500g/1lb 2oz natural yogurt
string or elastic band

1. Line a bowl with a piece of muslin cloth. Stir the salt into the yogurt before spooning it into the muslin-lined bowl. Bring the edges of the muslin together and tie into a tight bundle using string or an elastic band.

2. Hang the bundle over the bowl or hang it from the kitchen tap and leave it to drain for about 24 hours. By this time, most of the liquid will be lost and the resulting labneh will be beautifully thick and creamy.

3. Transfer from the muslin into a suitable container and store in the fridge, as you would yogurt, until ready to use.

GOCHUJANG INSPIRED RED CHILLI PASTE

MAKES
ABOUT
125G/4½OZ
V

Gochujang is a fermented red chilli paste that is a staple of Korean cuisine and it's well worth tracking down a jar of the original to fully appreciate its amazingly complex flavour. If you like kimchi, this one's for you. It can be used as a condiment, as we do in our bibimbap recipe, as a marinade, or a spoonful is a brilliant way of enhancing stews, soups and stir-fries. It's increasingly available in shops, but if you can't find it or are short of time this version, while it doesn't fully recreate the flavour of the real deal, still packs a delicious punch.

1 tbsp vegetable oil
1 small onion, chopped
2 cloves garlic, chopped
pinch of salt
2 tbsp sake
45g/1⅔ oz brown sugar
65g/2⅓ oz brown rice miso
1 tbsp chilli powder
1 tbsp brown rice vinegar

1. Heat the oil in a pan and sauté the onion for 3–5 minutes. Add the garlic and a pinch of salt and continue to sauté for a minute or so, before pouring in the sake and allowing to flambé.

2. Mix in the sugar and 3 tbsp of water and then stir in the miso paste too. Turn the heat down to low and continue to cook for a couple of minutes before adding in the chilli powder. Stir regularly as you continue to cook for a further 10–15 minutes, until it has begun to thicken. Add the rice vinegar and cook for another couple of minutes.

3. Leave to one side to cool, before transferring to a blender to combine into a smooth paste.

CHAPTER 6
BAKING AND
DESSERTS

BLUEBERRY COBBLER WITH LIME AND COCONUT

SERVES 6

240g/8½oz/scant 2 cups wholemeal self-raising flour

1 tsp baking powder

45g/1½oz/½ cup desiccated coconut

½ tsp salt

100g/3½oz/½ cup light muscovado or other unrefined brown sugar

115g/4oz/½ cup unsalted butter

grated zest and juice of 1 lime

½ tsp vanilla extract

250ml/9fl oz/1 cup whole milk

150g/5½oz/1 cup blueberries

cream or ice cream, to serve (optional)

This is a brilliant recipe to make in a cast-iron skillet, ideally one that's about 25cm/10in in diameter, but it can also be made in a baking tin greased with a little butter. It's super-easy to make and the ideal comfort food on a wintry day. It's definitely best served while still warm from the oven.

1. Preheat the oven to 180°C/350°F/Gas 4.

2. Put the flour and baking powder in a mixing bowl and add the coconut, salt and 85g of the sugar. Melt the butter in the skillet, then add it to the bowl along with the lime juice and zest, the vanilla and the milk. (Don't clean the skillet as the trace of butter will prevent sticking.) Mix thoroughly and transfer the mixture to the skillet.

3. Put the blueberries in a bowl and mix with the remaining sugar. Add the sugared blueberries to the skillet and place in the oven.

4. Bake for 35–40 minutes until golden brown around the edges. You can check whether it's cooked by poking it with a toothpick or skewer: if it comes out clean, it's ready. Serve with cream or ice cream.

BROWN SUGAR MERINGUES WITH ORANGE BLOSSOM AND SAFFRON CREAM AND FRESH RASPBERRIES

In our opinion, there's really nothing better than brown sugar meringues. They have a rich depth of flavour that white sugar simply can't match and are blissfully crisp on the outside while still being a bit chewy on the inside.

We make these meringues using an ice cream scoop as it's very neat and easy and gives a pleasing bun-like shape that can be cut in half to make cute meringue sandwiches. But it's fine to simply spoon them onto the baking tray, more rustic style, and you can use two meringues to make your sandwich, or load a single one up with toppings.

MAKES 8 MERINGUES
WF / GF

3 egg whites

pinch of salt

175g/6oz/generous ¾ cup soft light brown sugar

2 pinches of saffron

1 tbsp orange blossom water

300ml/10fl oz/1¼ cups double (heavy) cream

150g/5½oz/generous 1 cup raspberries

1. Preheat the oven to 120°C/250°F/Gas ½. Line a baking sheet with greaseproof (waxed) paper.

2. Whisk the egg whites with the salt until they stand in stiff peaks. Whisk in the sugar a spoonful at a time and continue whisking until the mixture is once again stiff.

3. Using an ice cream scoop, place scoopfuls of the mixture onto the lined baking sheet and place in the oven for 2–2½ hours until they're crisp.

4. Leave to cool on the baking sheet.

5. Just before serving, soak the saffron in the orange blossom water for about 10 minutes. Whip the cream until it forms soft peaks and then whisk in the orange blossom water and saffron.

6. Using a sharp serrated knife, cut each meringue in half. Place a spoonful of the cream and a few raspberries on the bottom half and sandwich with the top half.

COCONUT FLOUR BANANA BREAD

Dave's enjoyed banana bread since he was a young boy growing up in Zululand and picking his own bananas straight from the tree. This isn't quite the version his Mum used to make, but we love baking with coconut flour and it gives a nice twist to an old classic. Of course, it's better when the bananas are bordering on overripe (in South Africa, easily achieved by leaving them out in the sun). Feel free to replace the peanut butter with a nut butter of your choice. It's good with a bit of extra peanut butter on the side as a spread.

4 bananas

60g/2¼oz/¼ cup crunchy peanut butter

50g/1¾oz/¼ cup rapadura sugar or other unrefined brown sugar

½ tsp ground cinnamon

¼ tsp freshly grated nutmeg

½ tsp vanilla extract

120g/4¼oz/1 cup coconut flour

½ tsp bicarbonate of soda (baking soda)

½ tsp baking powder

pinch of salt

4 eggs

1. Preheat the oven to 180°C/350°F/Gas 4 and line a small loaf tin with greaseproof (waxed) paper.

2. Peel the bananas and place them in a large mixing bowl with the peanut butter, sugar, cinnamon, nutmeg and vanilla and mash it all up until it's well combined.

3. Sieve in the coconut flour, bicarbonate of soda, baking powder and salt, and fold in using a wooden spoon until thoroughly combined.

4. Beat 2 of the eggs together before folding them into the banana mixture. Then, separate the yolks from the whites of the 2 remaining eggs and, discarding the yolks, whisk the whites until they form stiff peaks, before gently folding them through the banana mixture too.

5. Transfer to the lined loaf tin and bake for about 40–45 minutes until it's thoroughly cooked (poke with a skewer and if it comes out clean it should be ready). Leave to cool in the tin for about 10 minutes before turning out and slicing.

RAW CACAO AND WALNUT ENERGY BALLS

MAKES
ABOUT
10 BALLS
V / WF / GF

These are super-straightforward, no-bake treats that we put together when we're craving something sweet in a hurry. Cacao powder is increasingly available in supermarkets as well as online and in health food shops and is one of our most-used ingredients. It's high in antioxidants, wonderfully mood-enhancing and capable of giving you a serious boost when your energy is a bit low.

150g/5½oz/1½ cups walnuts

100g/3½oz dates (ideally medjool), pitted

30g/1oz/⅓ cup cacao powder

½ tsp vanilla extract

4 tsp maple syrup

1. Put the walnuts in a food processor and blitz until they resemble breadcrumbs.

2. Divide the blitzed walnuts in half, return half of the walnuts to the food processor and blitz until they resemble a powder. Add the dates and blitz again until well combined. Add the cacao powder, vanilla, maple syrup and 1 tablespoon of water and blitz to combine well.

3. Add the remaining walnuts and pulse a few times until the mixture is combined but still has texture. Roll into balls and enjoy.

VEGAN CARROT HALWA

SERVES 4
V / WF / GF

500g/1lb 2 oz carrots, grated

350ml/12fl oz/scant 1½ cups almond milk

pinch of saffron

6 green cardamom pods, seeds only

1 tbsp coconut oil

60g/2oz/5 tbsp rapadura sugar or other unrefined brown sugar

60g/2oz/⅔ cup ground almonds

15 raisins

50g/1¾oz/½ cup flaked (sliced) almonds, toasted

This is a dessert we always look forward to when we're having an Indian meal. And it's so easy to make! Traditional versions use ghee, evaporated milk and whole milk, but we think this vegan version rocks. Why aren't carrots used in more desserts? *Illustrated overleaf.*

1. Put the carrots and almond milk in a large pan and bring it up to a simmer. Add the saffron and simmer for 20 minutes, stirring occasionally.

2. Meanwhile, crush the cardamom seeds. Stir them into the carrot mix and continue to simmer until the mixture starts to thicken, then add the coconut oil and sugar. Mix well and continue to cook until the mixture is fairly dry. Stir in the ground almonds and raisins and cook for a further 2–3 minutes.

3. Serve warm, topped with flaked almonds, or keep in the fridge for a day or so and serve cold.

SPICE-ROASTED NECTARINES WITH MASCARPONE

SERVES 2
VO / WF / GF

35g/1¼oz/2½ tbsp butter

2 star anise

1 cinnamon stick

½ tsp freshly grated nutmeg

1 tsp grated orange zest

30g/1oz/2 tbsp rapadura sugar
or other unrefined brown sugar

4 nectarines, cut in half,
stone removed

125g/4½oz/generous ½ cup
mascarpone, to serve

This is a super-easy one-pan dessert and is ideal for making in a cast-iron skillet, outdoors over a fire. Nectarines hold their shape well and look beautiful, but you can use many other kinds of fruit: peaches, plums, apples and pears are all great cooked in this way too.

1. Put the butter, star anise, cinnamon, nutmeg, orange zest and sugar in a skillet or heavy-bottomed frying pan over a medium heat until the butter has melted and the sugar dissolved, stirring regularly. Add the nectarines, cut side down, and cook for a couple of minutes. Add 3 tablespoons of water and continue to cook over a medium–high heat for 5 minutes. Flip the nectarines over and cook for another couple of minutes, stirring occasionally and flipping the nectarines over from time to time.

2. Serve with a generous spoonful of mascarpone.

Vegan option Omit the butter – you may need to add a little more water. Choose your favourite vegan cream or custard in place of the mascarpone.

SRI LANKAN COCONUT CUSTARD [WATALAPPAM]

SERVES 6
WF / GF

125ml/4fl oz/½ cup water
160g/5½oz/¾ cup rapadura sugar or other unrefined brown sugar
a little butter for greasing
400ml (1 can) coconut milk
8 cardamom pods, seeds only
½ tsp ground mace (or freshly grated nutmeg)
5 eggs
9 cashews, broken in half

We picked up this recipe on a trip to Sri Lanka. It's not unlike a crème caramel, but the flavour of coconut and the warming spices of cardamom and aromatic mace remind us that this is a version from the tropics. Ideally *watalappam* is made with *kitul jaggery*, a delicious form of jaggery made from the sap of a palm tree. It's dark and molasses-like and generally amazing, but it isn't easy to track down, so we suggest using rapadura or unrefined brown sugar.

1. Fill a roasting tray halfway with water and place in the oven. Set the oven to 150°C/300°F/Gas 2.

2. Put the water and 125g/4½oz/generous ½ cup of the sugar in a pan and bring to the boil over a medium heat, stirring occasionally. Once the sugar has completely dissolved, turn the heat up to high and cook for 10–12 minutes until the mixture thickens, the bubbles are smaller and you can smell caramel.

3. Pour an equal amount of the caramel into the bottom of six ramekins. Then lightly grease the sides of each ramekin above the caramel (be careful not to touch the caramel, it'll be very hot) and place them to one side to cool.

4. To make the custard, in a large bowl, mix the coconut milk with the remaining sugar until all the sugar has dissolved. In a pestle and mortar, grind the cardamom seeds to a powder and add to the coconut milk along with the mace; mix well.

5. Crack the eggs into a large bowl and whisk well. Pour the coconut mixture over the eggs and combine thoroughly. Pour this mixture into a jug and top up the ramekins, leaving a little room at the top. Place 3 cashew halves on top of each.

6. Carefully put the ramekins into the roasting tray in the oven and cook for 40–45 minutes. To check if they're done, poke the custard with a toothpick: if it comes out clean, it's ready; it should also have a little colour on the top.

7. Leave to cool completely, then cover with clingfilm (plastic wrap) and place in the fridge until you're ready to enjoy them. Loosen the sides of each ramekin with a small knife and then flip over onto a plate or bowl to serve.

RASPBERRY, ROSEWATER AND PISTACHIO FOOL

SERVES 4
WF / GF

This is a pud we rustle up for a quick dessert fix. You can make it solely with double cream but we find the addition of Greek yogurt makes it a little lighter. And we prefer it not super-sweet; you can add more sugar to the raspberries if you feel it needs it.

150g/5½oz/generous 1 cup raspberries
1½ tbsp unrefined brown sugar
1 tsp lemon juice
250ml/9fl oz/1 cup double (heavy) cream
150g/5½oz/⅔ cup Greek yogurt
2 tsp rosewater
30g/1oz/¼ cup pistachios, crushed

1. Put the raspberries, sugar and lemon juice into a pan and heat until the raspberries start to go soft. Mash with a fork until they're fully broken down and continue to heat for a minute or so. Place to one side to cool.

2. Whip the cream until it stands in stiff peaks, then gently fold in the yogurt.

3. Add the rosewater to the cooled raspberry mix and then gently fold it into the cream and yogurt, but not too thoroughly so as to keep a marbled effect.

4. Spoon into pots and place in the fridge to chill, or enjoy straight away. To serve, garnish with crushed pistachios.

WHOLEMEAL BUTTERMILK SKILLET SCONES

MAKES
ABOUT 12
SCONES

25g/1oz/2 tbsp butter, plus a little extra
for greasing
25g/1oz/2 tbsp unrefined soft brown sugar
1 egg
100ml/3½fl oz/scant ½ cup buttermilk
100g/3½oz/generous ¾ cup wholemeal
self-raising flour
pinch of salt

We love to make these when we're camping or on those happy occasions when we have access to an Aga. They're so simple and quick to make and are just heavenly served warm, straight from the skillet. Dripping with butter and honey is our personal preference but cream and jam are also yummy. Either way, make sure to have a piping hot cup of tea close to hand.

1. Cream the butter and sugar together in a mixing bowl. Mix in the egg and then mix in the buttermilk, sift in the flour and salt and mix well.

2. Warm the skillet or a heavy-bottomed frying pan over a low heat and then add a little butter to grease the bottom. Drop spoonfuls of the mixture into the skillet (we usually make 3–4 scones at a time), flatten each one slightly with the back of the spoon and then leave to cook for a couple of minutes until the underside is nicely coloured. Flip over and continue to cook until both sides are golden brown. Eat while still warm.

WHOLEFOOD DOG TREATS

MAKES
ABOUT 20

We had to include just one recipe designed for our furry best friend, Jaffa. These are his favourites; sometimes they even persuade him to come back to us when he's busy chasing a squirrel or having a good sniff around.

We were a bit sick of spending big bucks on not-that-great dog treats and it's so easy to make them yourself, giving you the added benefit of knowing exactly what's in them. Coconut oil is fantastic for dogs; not only for their skin and coats but it also helps to boost their digestive system and is a brilliant anti-parasitic. Woof!

100g/3½oz/1¼ cups porridge (rolled) oats

100g/3½oz/generous ¾ cup spelt flour, plus extra for rolling

1 tbsp coconut oil, melted

100g/3½oz/generous ⅓ cup crunchy peanut butter

1 banana, peeled and crushed

1 egg

1. Preheat the oven to 180°C/350°F/Gas 4. Line a baking sheet with greaseproof (waxed) paper.

2. Mix all the ingredients together in a large mixing bowl until well combined. Place the dough on a lightly floured surface and roll out to about 5mm/¼in thick. Use a cookie cutter (ideally a bone-shaped one) to cut into shapes and place on the baking sheet. Alternatively, divide the dough in half, roll each half into a sausage shape and use a sharp knife to slice off rounds.

3. Place in the oven for 25–30 minutes until nicely dried out. Leave to cool on a wire rack before training commences!

CHAPTER 7
DRINKS

GOLDEN MILK

MAKES ABOUT
500ML/18FL OZ/
2 CUPS (2 MUGS)
VO / WF / GF

We certainly can't take the credit for this ancient yogic drink, but it's one of our all-time favourite drinks and this is our preferred way of making it. More and more people are cottoning on to the benefits of turmeric – well known for centuries in the Ayurvedic tradition as being a powerful anti-inflammatory, great for your joints and brilliant for boosting liver function – and this is a great way to get lots of it into your diet. It's also a fantastic cappuccino substitute if you're trying to cut down on coffee.

You can prepare a larger quantity of the turmeric paste in advance as it keeps well in the fridge.

¼ tsp turmeric
125ml/4fl oz/½ cup water
500ml/18fl oz/2 cups almond milk
2 tbsp coconut oil
2 tsp honey or your choice of sweetener

1. Place the turmeric and water in a pan and bring to the boil. Boil for about 8–10 minutes or until it's formed a paste. Place to one side.

2. Slowly bring the almond milk and coconut oil to the boil; as soon as the milk comes to the boil, remove it from the heat. Stir in the turmeric paste and the honey and enjoy.

MILKY MASALA CHAI

MAKES
ABOUT 1 LITRE/
1¾ PINTS/4 CUPS
VO / WF / GF

It's worth a trip to India to sample this mighty brew in its homeland – nowhere else is it the same. One particular highlight was a chai wallah in Delhi whose skills with a teapot put some of our cocktail bartenders to shame (look him up on YouTube if you can't make the trip). We're serious chai drinkers. On a 10-day holiday to the lovely Yab Yum resort in Goa, we were alarmed when the bill at the end of our stay showed we'd consumed 65 pots! Back at home and suffering withdrawal symptoms (or perhaps just a sugar crash) we quickly had to learn how to make our own, and here's what we came up with.

To save time, you can make bigger batches of the chai spice mix and store it in an airtight container.

750ml/1¼ pints/3 cups water
250ml/9fl oz/1 cup whole milk, almond milk or soya milk
2 black tea bags
unrefined brown sugar, to taste (optional)

For the chai spice mix
1 tsp ground ginger
1 tsp ground cinnamon
1 tsp cloves
1 tsp ground black pepper
1 tsp green cardamom pods, seeds only
½ tsp freshly grated nutmeg

1. To make the chai mix, place a dry pan over a medium heat, add all the spices and toast for a couple of minutes until they become fragrant, moving them around occasionally to prevent burning. Leave to cool. Transfer to a coffee grinder or pestle and mortar and grind to a powder. Store in an airtight container.

2. When you're ready to enjoy your drink, place 1 teaspoon of the chai mix, the water, milk and teabags in a pan and bring to the boil. Reduce the heat and simmer for about 5 minutes. Strain and sweeten if desired before serving. (We like it sweet, as they have it in India, and usually put in 1 teaspoon – or even 2 – of sugar per cup.)

TIGER'S MILK

This is a powerhouse of a drink. Adapted from a recipe by Gayelord Hauser, a man widely acknowledged as one of the pioneers of natural eating, it contains brewer's yeast and blackstrap molasses, both of which are great for veggies as they're absolutely loaded with B vitamins and iron. Almond milk powder is also a super ingredient to get to know (we like the Ecomil brand) and we use it a bit like a protein powder or when we've forgotten to go the shops and run out of milk. If you can't find it or if you prefer to use dairy, the original version uses whole milk and skimmed milk powder. Ignore any curdling, this will make you strong!

SERVES 1
V / WF / GF

150ml/5fl oz/⅔ cup almond milk (or whole milk or any other milk of choice)
150ml/5fl oz/⅔ cup fresh orange juice
2 tsp almond milk powder
1 tsp brewer's yeast
1 tsp blackstrap molasses

Put all the ingredients in a blender and blend until smooth. Enjoy over ice if you like.

GREEN HEAVY METAL DETOX SMOOTHIE

MAKES
ABOUT 750ML/
1¼ PINTS/3 CUPS
V / WF / GF

500ml/18fl oz/2 cups coconut water

1 banana, peeled

1 date, pitted

50g/1¾oz spinach

60g/2oz kale, stalks removed

1 bunch (about 25–30g, including stalks)
coriander (cilantro)

These days, almost all of us are exposed to toxic amounts of heavy metals that accumulate within the body and can lead to all sorts of health issues. But help is at hand. Coriander is a top detox ingredient and it is the star of this green smoothie. These drinks are the ultimate in fast food and a great way to get a mega hit of nutrition with hardly any bother. You can also add a teaspoon of spirulina, wheatgrass or chlorella (available from health food shops) if you really want to amp it up.

Put the coconut water, banana, date, spinach, kale and coriander leaves in a blender and blend for a couple of minutes until smooth. We prefer it served over ice but the more hardcore can enjoy it straight from the blender.

LEMON BARLEY WATER

MAKES ABOUT
300ML/10FL OZ/
1¼ CUPS (2 SMALL
GLASSES)
V

This is an old-fashioned number but it's such a comforting one – a bit like getting a good hug. Steeping grains such as barley in water to make a drink is a practice that can be traced back to the ancient Greeks, and they were definitely onto something as it's a real health tonic: high in fibre and B vitamins (great for us veggies), as well as many other vitamins and minerals – and revered for giving a beautiful complexion to all who drink it. To maximize the nutritional benefits, look for barley flakes made from hulled rather than pearl barley. We enjoy it over ice but you can also serve it warm; even, dare we say, with a wee drop of brandy, for medicinal purposes of course! It can also be diluted to taste with extra water if you find it too strong.

100g/3½oz/1¼ cups barley flakes
2 tbsp unrefined brown sugar
2 lemons, halved
600ml/20fl oz/2½ cups boiling water

1. Put the barley flakes into a jug along with the sugar, the juice from the lemons and the lemon halves. Pour over the boiling water and stir well, then cover and leave to cool.

2. Once cool, strain, giving the lemon halves a final squeeze.

SWITCHEL

MAKES
2 LITRES/
3½ PINTS
V / WF / GF

Switchel is a traditional woodsman's drink, otherwise known as haymakers' punch, that has recently been appropriated by hip Brooklynites, keen to lock down its thirstquenching, super-refreshing taste and its many health benefits. Switchel is brilliant for restoring electrolytes (move over coconut water, although we still love you, too) and it is hands down the most palatable way we've found of drinking apple cider vinegar. Try to use an unfiltered apple cider vinegar as this will contain traces of the 'mother', the murky debris found at the bottom of the bottle, which contains huge amounts of proteins, enzymes and good bacteria.

You can use honey in place of maple syrup if you prefer.

2 litres/3½ pints/2 quarts water (ideally filtered)

50g/1¾oz fresh root ginger, finely chopped

juice of 1 lemon

4 tbsp apple cider vinegar (ideally organic and unfiltered)

6 tbsp maple syrup

1. Put the water into a 2.5 litre/4½ pint/2½ quart preserving jar. Add the ginger, lemon juice, vinegar and maple syrup, seal and shake. You can enjoy it immediately over ice but it's even better if you leave it in the fridge to brew for 12–24 hours.

2. Before drinking, taste and add a little more lemon juice or maple syrup if you like.

INDEX

ACKNOWLEDGEMENTS

Our huge and heartfelt thanks go to everyone at Pavilion for making this book happen. To Emily Preece-Morrison, Senior Commissioning Editor, for sharing our vision for this book over coffee and then making it a reality – thank you so much! And to Laura Russell and Claire Clewley for such brilliant design, we're thrilled. Big thanks too to Maggie Ramsay for helping us so much with the copy-editing.

We felt so lucky to work again with the incredible photographers Liz and Max Haarala Hamilton. The photography is, as always, just amazing. And we're so grateful to Alexander Breeze for prop styling and to Alex Gray for food styling. We couldn't have wished for a more brilliant and talented team and you've all made this book such a pleasure to create. We'll never forget lugging all that gear up into the woods in Cumnor and hope there'll be a chance for more outdoors adventures together someday. We loved spending time with you all.

We're also eternally grateful for all the support of our families. To both sets of parents, who we know are behind us every step of the way. To Mama/Miranda, who started the whole vegetarian ball rolling and knew all about wholefoods long before it started getting trendy. To Dad/Michael who we know is always ready to help out with any madcap endeavour. And to Mum/Wilma and Dad/Doug for sharing their love of good food and for getting Dave into catering college all those years ago.

Thank you also to all the family and friends who've braved helping us out in the van, we warned you it could be hardcore! To Ellie, Kai, Kev, Taryn and to Evie for her incredible slogans. And to all the other amazing people who have worked with us over the years: especially to Fatih and Yakup, Charlie and Jess, Tom and Charlotte, Louis and Gee.

We're super grateful to Islington council for our pitch at the brilliant Whitecross Street and to all the event organisers who've involved us in the most fabulous happenings over the years. And we just can't thank enough our wonderful and loyal Buddha Bowl Van customers. Your support means so much to us and it makes us so happy that you enjoy what we do.

Finally, we can't forget our lovely doggie Jaffa, who makes everything more fun and gets us into the great outdoors even more often than we otherwise would.

First published in paperback in the United Kingdom in 2019 by
Pavilion
43 Great Ormond Street
London
WC1N 3HZ

ISBN 978-1-911624-09-7

A CIP catalogue record for this book is available from
the British Library.

10 9 8 7 6 5 4 3 2 1

Reproduction by Mission, Hong Kong
Printed and bound by 1010 Printing International Ltd, China

www.pavilionbooks.com